CW01481533

# Canto Libri

## by Birri Sangha

authorHOUSE®

AuthorHouse™
1663 Liberty Drive
Bloomington, IN 47403
www.authorhouse.com
Phone: 1-800-839-8640

Published by AuthorHouse 6/26/2012

ISBN: 978-1-4772-1467-1 (sc)
ISBN: 978-1-4772-1468-8 (e)

*Acknowledgements*

*Dear AJ and Gaurika,*
*Thank you for your untiring efforts for help in*
*bringing these thoughts together.*
*You were the needle and thread in bringing all the chapters together*

*"Canto Libri"*
*Canto (Latin) means "to sing" and libri means "book" -*
*canto libri translates as "songbook" or "hymnal."*

*A **hymn** is a song… religious, written with praise, adoration or prayer*
*in heart and mind. Collection of hymns is known as hymnals.*

*Each life is a songbook; my life, too. This is my songbook; One Chapter*
*of my journey so far. I am sure there are many more Chapters to come;*
*many more Chapters to share and share I will …With total openness.*

*Each song a sacred hymn; each breath a precious pearl;*
*some one somewhere has been kind on my world.*

*My life is a songbook… sung in full by some…few… but mostly in part by*
*many…My songbook will remain…for always…Canto Libri is one song…*
*one chapter of my life…Come share My Canto Libri, My Hymnal…*

*We are all connected….like the words in a sentence;*

*God has made sure …all beads stay in one rosary; the rosary of life*

*Like the sentences making up the paragraph;*

*Like the paragraphs making up the chapter; the*
*chapters making up the whole story…*

*I am where I am by design. God is the master architect. I am*
*here by Destiny. I am meant to be here, precisely here.*

*City to City; Heart to Heart; Lifetime to Lifetime, Some stories appear*
*to have no beginnings; some no middle or the interesting interlude*
*and some no ending. I have found that all stories are complete within*
*themselves. It is just a matter of perception and understanding. How you*
*see something defines what it becomes. The eye is our greatest Judas; it*
*is the eye that makes a soul fly and it is the eye that makes a soul die*

*All the stories that make up the rosary…My Canto Libri….*
*are here open to your eye and heart to read…and sing….*

# 1. Born Prodigal

*We are all born more or less...prodigal.*

*It is only when we do our first act of kindness...We find meaning...*

*How late I have left finding meaning in my life...*

*All of us are born prodigal...but some of us will die that way, too*

*I have taken so much for granted...*
*I take each breath as if I had right to it...*

*So many breaths have been taken...*
*I wonder how many remain.*
*Each rosary has its own beads...*
*I wonder how long is the rosary...my chain*

*I wonder how much remains...*
*Before Nature claims back the chain...*

## 2. Purpose

*How do I find out the purpose of my life?*
*Who should I ask?*
*"Dear Heart we all conceal...*
*Open up and reveal...*
*Peel away the onion rings...*
*throw away your mask...*
*How does it feel?*
*When you expose...all that you are...and reveal?"*

*"I have to make the journey to the core...*
*and feel the ocean rolling over my soul...*
*I just can't do that...standing on the shore...*
*the purpose of life is to explore...something more...Have you found more?"*

## 3. Give It Away

*How do you give it away when you want to give away the lot...?*
*How do I give away more than what is in my life's pot...?*
*I mean give away more than what I've got...?*

*All the oceans, lakes, rivers and streams...*
*How do I give away my heart and soul and all my dreams...?*
*All the summer skies, quiet white clouds and gentle rain fall*
*How do I give away this all...?*

*All my meadows, gardens and quiet ponds...*
*How do I go beyond...*
*the normal thing...?*
*How do I give away everything..?.*

*My bibles, poetry, music and the library of prayers...*
*How do I share?*
*Eternity and space...*
*and all the joy on my face...*

*How do I simply empty out all my pockets, closets, wardrobes, suitcases*
*and holdall...?*
*How do I make that call?*

*I have held back all my life...Let me change...*
*to make the jigsaw complete...I need to rearrange...*
*a piece here and there...*
*with threads of love and care...*

*I have wasted a lifetime*
*I have measured and counted return*
*I have read so many libraries of books*
*and yet one thing I have yet to learn...*

*"Dear Heart... When will you learn to pour...?*
*Where it all comes from there is so much more...*
*Learn to open that door..."*

*Let me give it all away...today...*
*"Take what you need and more...*
*Yes...Dear Heart I'm sure"*

*An Afterthought*
*It is on the darkest night...I need the most light...*
*to guide me and be the Captain inside me*

# 4. God Listens

*I have said quiet prayers for my family...friend...strangers...and me*

*God does listen....*
*Have you noticed how he listens and hears...everything and everyone...?*
*"Dear Heart...Go ahead...Whisper the prayer in your soul..."*

*My prayers have been answered kindly...and granted...many times*

*Dear God you do listen...*

*I have often wondered who dries the tears cried...*

*in solitude and deserts of life...*

*You are the kind breeze that touches every cheek and eye*

*seeking love and direction....*

*"Which way is home?"*

*"This way....Dear Heart...this way...there ...*
*Follow the direction of your prayers"*

## 5. Pebbles in my Mind

There are pebbles
floating in my mind...
some sharp and cutting
some blunt and kind...
Which pebble are you?
Any pebble just wouldn't do

There are stones
sinking in my soul...
some crushing it to pieces
some paving it back to whole...
Which stone are you?
Any stone just wouldn't do.

Some waves take the floating autumn leaves
further down the stream...
And some crash them back to an unfriendly shoreline
sinking in their own dreams...
Which wave are you?
Any wave just wouldn't do...
I am seeking a wave...warm and true
Are you?

There are rocks
flowing in my heart
some soft and soothing
some tearing it apart
which rock are you?
Any rock just wouldn't do...

I am a weary traveller...
I need a place to sleep and rest...Let me lay close to your heart and chest
I've had so many pillows
made from rocks and stones and weeping willows
the feeling has grown
and grows even faster...when the soul is alone
at the crossroads...asking and pleading
"I am badly needing
directions home"

There are mountains
falling on my fragile skin
Some melting in to gentle raindrop
some piercing in... And falling deep within

Let me rest a while
and catch my breath...
Before the rosary is broken
by life's Macbeth...
Which royal soul are you?
Any soul just wouldn't do...
I seek only a soul that true
Are you?

## 6. A Man Defined

A man is defined by...
moulded and refined by...
skinned or lined by...
the inner fire and its intensity...
the soul, its inertia and density

I am no more than my intentions...
All that I am...I am a reflection of my intentions and the fire
the passion and desire...

I hold no residue....You are forgiven...
I pray that you forgive me too
I hope I have never...known or unknown to me...wronged you...

I wish shelter and protection for soul and heart...
May they always be embraced by life...and never torn apart...
by shallow intentions of breezes unkind...
May the breeze always leave springtime in your eyes
and never leave a tear fall that leaves you temporarily...or permanently blind

Some seasons can leave a heart torn and broken
And some can also leave the soul suspended in
words silently spoken...or unspoken

The secret is to keep...your soul deep in the innermost of cores
Where only God Captains all the shores...

*Keep your intentions focussed and pure*
*When under stress and strain...Learn to endure...*
*and rise...with Horizon in your eyes*

*Guard your intentions from breezes wishing to corrupt and destroy*
*and when you feel that you are sinking...Build your own buoys*
*and learn to float...*
*and then to fly...*
*It is your thoughts that'll make you soar or die...*

*Die you not, dear heart...You were born to rise...*
*I can see God leaving wings in your wintered eyes...*

*Somewhere... in the gentle rain ...and soft white snow...*
*I can see your spirit nourish and grow....*
*Life is a garden...that your intentions must hoe...*
*Before a rich harvest can grow*
*Learn to keep your intentions pure....*
*Let no other soul corrupt...or disrupt...your learning*
*the greatest lessons are learnt when the soul and the heart are churning...*
*All diamonds are chiselled from coal...*
*and so it is with great hearts and souls*

## 7. How often we Speak

How often we speak...
mostly hi's and bye's...
Our relationship is like the outer ribbons and ties...
Oh...the gift we hide...deep inside...
to know someone deeply...
My soul wants to know who it knows completely...
I am not a man seeking just the outer skin...
I want to know what lies within...

If I am to know you...Let me know you deeply...
I mean let me in to your soul...
Let me know you completely....

The morning breeze that skimmed the early morning dew...
Never knew...
Just what lies further in...?
Where the true blossoms begin...

Next time we speak...
Let us talk deeply...
And say it all, the way it is
and get to know each other completely

## 8. The Dog can hear your Heartbeat

*I lost my dog in a small town...*
*outside Indiana....somewhere*
*running around like a madman*
*searching frantically everywhere*

*Couldn't sleep...*
*cried all night*
*searching by daylight*
*searching by starlight*
*high and low*
*low and high...*
*Where? How? Why?*

*I came across an old man sleeping on the street*
*Kind enough to guide me:*
*" Did you know that dogs can hear your heart beat...?*
*Slow down...be calm. Be still*
*Hear your heartbeat, he will"*

*I lay myself on the bench*
*and slowed my soul down to a still*
*there in the quiet*
*I found my lost fill*
*I heard a bark...I heard a hum*
*My Lucy ran towards me and hugged away the numb...*
*Some kind soul... Some kind heart*
*Found and took her in ...when we came apart...*
*"I owe you a debt of gratitude, my friend...*
*Tell me where these heart felt prayers I should send"*

## 9. An Honest Man

He was an honest man.
Who corrupted him?
An ocean flowing...
Who disrupted him?
From the man that he was
to the man that he became...
Who fractured a heart of porcelain... a soul of steel...?
Who is to blame?
Tell me your name...

He was a kind man.
Who made him cold?
An ageless soul...
What made him suddenly old?
An evergreen heart
to a barren and empty space...
Who crushed a soul of porcelain...and a heart of gold...?
Which heartless face?
Which heartless face?

He had weights on his shoulders
and heavy on his heart
both the weights and the heavy
took him apart...
The price he paid
for being a caring heart...
A heart of fractured pieces...
A soul of shattered parts...

I wonder if anyone will miss him.
Although today you all cried...
A mountain of a soul
on his own when he died......
Life is a passing thing...
How quickly it fades...
All the sunshine it brings...
goes back into the shades
like patches of desert in glades.

He was a loving man...
How did he become insane?
If he was loved in return
where are the remains?
Not a single grain...
only anguish and pain...
He was immaculate...
Who left their stains?
Own up...
What is your name?

## 10. He

He was a family man
what went wrong?

"Someone changed the music...
and it all became a different song"

He was an honest man
what went wrong?

"Someone rearranged the values...
and all his old values no longer belong"

He was a caring man
where did it all go wrong?

"Someone ignored his heart
and his heart wasn't that strong"

Someone took over his soul...
and left their clouds there...
And he lost all his light...
somewhere...
And when it was all said and done
there was no one there
who really cared...
They all left their monkeys on his shoulders...
No one asked:
"Why is he getting weaker and weaker by the day...
Are these all our boulders?
Why are they all on his shoulders?"

Real wisdom is not to learn the lesson after its all gone wrong
but to learn them long before
someone loses all reason and rhyme
and the keys to the door...
We all learn...
Either when the bridge has fallen...
or when it has started to burn..?
And then we mourn and cry...
Inconsolable....Dear Heart why?
Why did you not see?
Long ago...How it should be?

If there is to be a conversation...
it has to be today...
before our differences get any stronger...
and the distance stretched longer
and the bridge...burns away...
leaving voids and deep gaps between our hearts...
and our relationship...simply falls apart...

Life is brief...
these blossoms...are beautiful...
Why throw in an autumn leaf?

## 11. J

*I wish I knew...*
*What to do...?*

*I've been here countless times before...*
*standing outside your door...*
*begging mercy and pardon*
*May I take some seeds for my parched and struggling garden...*

*You throw away more than I'll see in my lifetime...*
*I drink from the half finished bottles from yesterday...*
*You always over fill...over spill*
*so many times...*
*how you waste wine*

*I don't ask for much....just a touch of love will do...*

*My only wish... not to lose what is mine*
*I don't mind sharing all my vineyards and the wine...*
*You don't like giving back...*
*It's something you lack...*
*You take and take*
*till the vineyard bankrupts and breaks...*
*and even then I hear your "I"*
*with total disregard for the struggle in my eye*

## 12. Some Souls

Some souls are like a fire
they warm all...
asking for no reasons or qualifications
or how they roll the ball...
Yes...they warm all

Some souls are like an endless candle
with their never ending light
they seek those in shadows and darkness
they seek the endless night
to share their light

Some souls are like a universe
enclosed within some bone and skin
there's a universe within a universe within a universe
to discover when you journey in
the wonders of the universe within

Some souls are like an endless blue sky
with hidden warm drops of kind rain
they seek those with cuts and bruises
and heal them again
and rain away pain

Some souls when they die
they don't really die
You can see them clearly
shinning thru' some ones eyes
teaching all souls to fly

*Some souls when they pass other souls*
*recognise missing parts*
*Soul to Soul …merging together*
*heart beats and hearts*

*Some souls are like water*
*ocean and sea*
*always there*
*where some soul needs them to be*
*kind and caring*
*simply sharing*

*Some souls give it all away*
*all their pearls and gold*
*never listen to those advising*
*"Dear Heart save some for when you get old"*

*"Consider it dear life I've been told…*
*I still want to share my gold"*

*I have you sleeping here by my side*
*these trees have been kind on our skin…*
*Dear Soul even these meadows*
*hold a beautiful universe within…*
*openly sharing*
*kind and caring…*
*asking for no reason or rhyme*
*simply sharing beautiful space and time*

*I have met many souls*
*and I have loved them all*
*Some held my hand whilst I was walking*
*and some offered it to me when they saw me fall*
*yes...Dear Life I have loved them all*
*Some souls touch you so deeply*
*and when you look within the deep*
*You realise they were always there with you*
*sharing with your soul, dreams and restful sleep*

*Some souls are like a bible*
*full of hymns and prayer*
*and when you look into their eyes*
*you find your bible there*
*the bible you've been searching for everywhere*
*the bible I lost somewhere...*

*Some souls touch you so deeply...and completely*
*colouring the canvass rich and bright*
*"Dear Heart ...Dear Soul....You are my Painter...Brush in your Heart light"*

## 13. Losses & Crosses

How does a heart heal?
How does it learn to re-feel?
We all learn to calm our hearts...
We learn to bandage and balm our hearts...
There is no other way...
We are all actors in Life's play...

I need to learn to fly...
I know I got my wings somewhere in my eye...
The Captain deep inside me, waiting to guide me...

The soul learns to carry all its crosses...
And all the grief and losses
it learns to be...
The Captain it needs for the seas...
God leaves enough strength in all
to knock down...rebuild the walls
Tsunami hits all souls...
All Tsunami's take their toll...
In leaving only tears and losses...
Let the Japanese souls be blessed and kindly caressed
with courage to bear all their losses...and crosses

## 14. The Ducklings

*The mother duck tried to run back to the water*
*the crow saw it all...struggling duckling at the*
*back...with one dive...caught her*
*there were three and then only two*
*I wonder if the mother knew....*
*And then only one...after a moment none...*

*I saw the mother searching in vain...*
*I cried a quiet tear...I felt its pain*
*like a knife and salt on a wound that will never heal*
*I wonder how the stitches and the crow feels?*
*Will it ever be revealed?*
*Or do you simply endure*
*the pain that is yours?*
*I wonder if Mother Nature ever cries...When something dies*

## 15. Peter and Paul

*What is the distance between distance and nearness?*
*Just how close is the nearness between closeness and distance?*

*Peter was all gentle warmth to start...the closer one became the*
*greater the fire... till finally all who came close singed or got burnt*

*that's the way he was made...born to singe and*
*burn all beautiful wings and petals...*

*I enjoyed his intensity and density....but I too experienced*
*singed soul...smoking dreams and values*
*All I have left from knowing him... a hand full of dust and ashes...*
*I don't think he cared much of what I thought...or how I felt.*
*All that mattered to him ...How quickly he finished*
*off the dilapidation and dismantle*
*after the first brick was torn away*

*Peter always thought he was the Master of everything...anything. He was.*
*But he always forgot or forgot to remember at the*
*opportune moments that Paul was wiser...*
*having more years in his skin and bones...and wisdom*
*comes with age...and he was older. One was smart; the other*
*wiser but neither knew... How deceptive life can be?*

*What is the distance that separates age...?*
*Are time and the ticking of a timer a reasonable measure*
*of difference between two rings on a tree trunk?*
*What if the younger soul lived twice as much in its younger life?*
*And what if an older soul wasted away all their time...realising only on*
*the day of reconciliation and settlement what fool they were and been?*
*Will they be punished...or will they be counselled and*
*tutored how to spend wisely...if not money...time?*

*What separates me from you?*
*We are different colour...But are we really different?*
*Is the tone of our skin enough to force us to stay apart... enough*
*to claim that we are from two different countries...?*
*When you go back home, which sea or ocean do*
*you sail and cross to reach home?*
*Or are we all simply going home...ignorant of*
*the fact we are same colour souls...*
*Will you expose your soul long enough for me to compare and take notes...?*
*How close we are even at a distance and how far*
*apart we are when sharing a handshake*

*Some hearts will share your heart and maybe even spend a few*
*summers there and yet still be million miles away...apart.*
*What invisible walls separate these hearts?*
*Paul always stands apart...even when he shares the music from your heart...*
*He has mastered the art...of being close and apart at the same time...*
*Clever man...? I am nor sure...not anymore.*
*I have seen him struggling between two shores trying*
*to stand on both shores at the same time.*

*I have seen the sky question a rainbow: "How*
*far are you from my heart beat?"*
*"I am only as far as you think I am...and close as you feel I am"*

# 16. Sunrise

*I want to see sunrise in your eyes*
*How beautiful that would be*
*You, Dear Life...shinning life on me*

*I want to spend the day with you*
*How wonderful that would be*
*You, Dear Heart...spending your day with me*

*Life comes and life goes*
*sometimes it flows...sometimes it doesn't flow*
*Seasons run in circles*
*some in tune*
*You are all my seasons in June*

*I want to see*
*the sunset thru' your heart*
*How amazing that would be*
*You, Dear Soul...sharing your heart with me*

*The sun rises..and then sets*
*Only few remember but most will forget*
*that's how it all flows*
*I've been around a lifetime*
*my heart knows...*
*love is what matters*
*only love remains*
*I am all stains Dear Love ...*
*colour pure in to all my stains*

*I want to spend my life with you*
*How rich and fulfilling that would be*
*You, Dear love loving all your love, with me.*

## 17. A Soul at Soul Crossing

I am a soul at soul crossing
tired of the turning and the tossing
losing my way again…the crossroads have not been kind friends.

Some roads were unkind
some punched my soul so hard…And. left me almost blind…

I am a soul at soul crossing
white flag in my pocket…guiding back the loss in
into my days…
before I get lost again and go astray…

Which road should I take?
Which road has a lesser heartache?
Which road with no intentions to break?
A soul weary and tired
Beaten by the storms…
left picking up the pieces…left empty and uninspired…

I am a soul at a soul crossing
seeking a kind harbour to anchor the loss in
and take some rest…and put some songs back into my chest
to sing whenever I need to
Am I going to be one of those lucky few…?

There's a window in the distance…
someone's calling me from…
Is this where I need to be?
Is this where I belong?

I am a soul at soul crossing…
too tired to even raise a white flag
of surrender…
to some kind soul…warm and tender
Let me in….I am in the middle of nowhere…let me re-begin.
I am a soul at a soul crossing

## 18. Cuttings

Take my soul...take a cutting and plant me
let the gardens in your heart want me...
Dear Heart ....want me...
Let me feel your love in how you plant me....

Take my heart...take a grafting and bind me
let the meadows in your soul find me...
Dear Soul.... find me...
Let me feel your love in how you bind me...

Like a river flowing to the sea
waiting on blossoms drying or dry
Dear Life
Come, fill my eye

Take my Life...take a moment from these moments
Let the moment shine me
I am a harvest...waiting on kind season
shield and mine and re-mine me

## 19. Am I?

*How can I be untrue?*
*When all I love is you…*

*How can that be?*
*When all that I am is what you have loved in to me…*

*Have I lied?*
*When all I hold…is you inside…*

*You say I have been untrue…*
*You are perfectly right…*
*You are not my day*
*But both my day and night…*

*Dismantle me dear life…I need to expose*
*the heart that beats within this enclose*
*Am I a thorn…or a thorn on a rose?*
*Expose….Dear Life… Expose…*

*Whatever I am…I am for you*
*if that is untrue…then I am untrue*
*All that I am…*
*Will be a lie of a man…?*

*Dear God you are my witness…*
*Tell me…No…Shout it out:*
*"Am I untrue?"*

*"Dear Heart…only if your heart is not beating within you….*
*Listen to the beat…*
*If it is incomplete…you are incomplete…*
*If it is complete…You will hear integrity in every heartbeat*
*all that I hear…."You are all that is dear""*

## 20. Searching

*I lay there from early morning to late evening*
*totally exposed to the sea waves...*
*the sunbathers silence*
*and self reflection...*
*Which wave am I waiting on to roll on my skin...?*
*How the waves begin...one after another how they roll in*
*and then subside...*
*When it does, has that wave died?*
*Or only changed texture and tone...its skin and bone...*
*Are all waves all alone?*
*Is each wave a wave on its own?*
*Or are they... are we all connected by an invisible thread or tie...?*
*Can we connect with just eyes?*
*Or do we have to share something deeper than a mere touch?*
*I have felt a touch that had so much...*

*I lay there day in day out...slept away a full*
*week of God granted time and life.*

*I came back late Sunday and on Monday morning at about 7am*
*I actually missed the early morning soothing of the waves and the sea...*
*I should lie on quiet beaches more often...*
*The rest made me realise I am only a fragile human soul...*
*needing replenishing...*
*and caring for...*
*We search all our life....and sometimes still cannot find the*
*one wave that will dress and balm our skin and soul...*
*Why?*
*What are you searching for dear heart...dear eye?*

## 21. Fisherman

*Like the Fisherman searching the sea*
*I too was searching for me...*

*Like the fisherman too blind to see*
*I too was blind as can be*

*I looked in the mirror to see...*
*But I couldn't see me...*
*I couldn't see beyond the skin*
*I was interested in what was within*
*Have I a soul?*
*Is it all a lie?*
*Is my Judas in my eye?*

*Like the fisherman who found fish all around*
*I too found*
*Me*
*in all that I now see*

*I am precisely where I'm meant to be?*
*Dear Life you chose these coordinates for me...*
*So hold my soul in your eye and guide me...*
*Be the Captain inside me*

*I was searching...and I have found...*
*God in my soul...and also all around*
*Dear God embrace me...*
*I am losing outline retrace me...*
*Redefine me...I am an unmined mine, mine me*

## 22. Shadow Free

I have searched...
maybe in vain...?
Some times the harvest you have lost
has lost all its fruits and grain...
the reason you can't find them... is because nothing remains

I have searched the colours of rainbows
in all rain falls...
I thought I'd find something
But I found nothing at all...
All I found in some rain falls...was just a rainfall

I have searched the clouds above the mountain
and questioned the clouds:" Where can it be?"
The clouds quietly whispered:
"Why ask me?
I am also searching...searching high and low
and the only answers I found:
learn to rain out and flow"

I have searched behind the sunshine
But all I found was the sun...
shinning in all directions
questioning the shadows behind every one...
"Do you seek to be....shadow free?
If you do...let me shine on you from every way...
and you'll be shadow less by end of the day....
All I desire....that you stay open to embrace life and its fire"

I searched and searched...until the night embraced my soul in its quiet skin...
and I found million rainbows...
in my soul within...

All rainbows are colours made from your intentions...
I am a reflection of my intentions and nothing more...
I decide....Am I less than a grain of sand ...or the whole shore?

## 23. How Quickly

How quickly it all changes...
Life is a continuous process...How it rearranges...
The piece that used to fit here...fits no more...that is clear...

We all grow...while we flow
in the river of life and all its streams...
Some waves are meant to salt the wound...
Some sent to stitch and heal the seams...

Am I here to learn....How to let go...gracefully...accepting "What is..."?

I can hear God whispering in my soul:
"All relationships I create with a purpose of learning...
Some bridges will fall and die early…
Others will be always remaining even with all its ties burning...
We come alone...We all leave the same...
Taking with us only the learning...all else remains...here...
Some memories will bring rainbow to the glistening eye...
And some add more storms and colour more loneliness in to the tear...

Let all that remains… recall...YOU brought joy to them all"

The silent Robin nesting deep in the branches of the tree...
constantly humming:
"Dear Life....You have always been kind to me...
The rain that is warm and kind...
How and when does it gain its will to tear down all that comes in its way....
Making even the eagle that yesterday soared high...
Today sit silent seeking answers for the many
unanswered questions in its eyes...:
"Am I here to learn...What am I here to learn?
Before the road whispers: "It's time to return""""

*Let me stand here a little longer...*
*This rain is kind on my body and soul...*
*I feel stronger*
*I will take my time...and with knowing walk slowly...*
*I want the rain to get to know me...*

*"Let me learn all I need to learn...and journey across*
*all the bridges...long burnt or still burning...*

*The greatest learning comes when the body and*
*the soul are at their most vulnerable...*
*And I stand here exposing my heart and soul today....*
*The choice is yours....*
*Save and guide me over these bridges...or*
*knowingly allow me to lose my way.*
*"What's it to be....Dear God...Make your decision on me"*

## 24. Missing Shoe

*We are all searching…*
*Some for missing shoe*
*some the missing soul…*
*how some missing leave a gaping hole*
*I have drained away…*
*almost rained away*
*I guess what remains…are the few final frames…*

*Where is our friendship gone?*
*Has it moved on?*
*When it dies, how does it die?*
*And when it leaves our eyes, how does it leave our eye?*
*Why?*

*How do you console…a soul*
*left with missing and holes*
*torn apart*
*all the sinews of the souls and heart*

*I recall the choice*
*But God knows the anguish*
*I lost both my soul and voice:*

*"It would be more humane to put her down*
*surrender her skin and soul to the ground"*

*"I know the ground would be kinder*
*my dilemma is…How will I ever find her….Again…?*
*My dear, dear friend…*
*All things come*
*All things go*
*Where or when?*
*No one knows…*
*And I miss her…yes, I do*
*Just where she's gone*
*I wish I knew"*

*Where is our friendship gone?*
*They say all seasons move on...and you too have moved on*
*I go searching deep in the meadows hoping to hear....*
*Your voice in one of my tears*

*All relationships form here...*
*and this where we cry all our tears...*
*Empty handed we come...*
*We leave the same*
*the coming and the going*
*is all that remains...*
*Some leaves fall and get blown away*
*and some stay to experience another day*

*Dear God explain to me why?*
*Some souls never leave our eye?*
*How they merge with the colours of our soul...*
*And when gone*
*leaving missing and empty hole...*
*How do I console...my soul?*

*"Where is our friendship gone?"*

*"Dear Heart...I have moved on*
*But remember this I am not gone...*
*I am still in your heart and soul*
*Let my love bandage and balm you...*
*console and calm you*
*and whole you...and re-soul you*
*I am not gone...only moved on*
*I am still here…in all your smiles and tears"*

## 25. Drunk

I went to bed sober last night...
And yet I woke up drunk...
the early morning breeze is like a vineyard on my body...and soul

I love this early morning hour ...
I have yet to figure out why I rise so early every morning...
regardless of how late I went to bed the night before...

I dare not miss the special sunrise...in your honey eyes…
Like the petals that make love with the bee...
Your early morning eyes make love with me....

The silence between us has its warmth...and words …
"Dear Life...It is your love that saved me from getting lost at the crossroads...
And crossroads there were many...
You are the reason...I am...I am...
And I have been in love with you...All this lifetime...
And any other lifetimes that I may have enjoyed before

I wake up drunk...sleeping next to your blanket warm skin...

There is intoxication...in your embrace....
Let me drink all night...
I want to wake up drunk all my remaining days
If this is what love does to the soul and skin…Dear Life let me live forever.…

And if I am to die…Let me die sharing love in your eyes

## 26. Jigsaw

There's a jigsaw
I would love to solve
I've been evolving a lifetime
and yet still I am reluctant to evolve
How will I solve what I was born to solve...?

"Dear Heart....be open to direction....learn to evolve"

There are pieces missing
I cannot find
I know I left them somewhere...behind

"Where or when…Only you know…Can't help you my friend…"

Should I travel back in time
and say what I should've long said...?
Or what's gone is gone...and no more
Are all yesterdays gone and dead?

"The answers are all inside your heart and head"

There are some pieces...
of which there are more than one
So many rays of feint sunshine
No sign of a sun
Dear Heart what have you done...?

"When you turned away from the summer, the winter begun"

*There are so many square pegs in round holes.*
*How can that be?*
*So many square pegs and round holes in me!*
*Should I file away the sharp corners?*
*And blunt away the sharp and cold?*
*Dear Life ...I feel young*

*"How long will the soul survive in skin and bones ...fast getting old?"*

*"I have been so blind all my life...*
*Saw no difference between silver and gold …*
*That's how I bought and sold!*
*I must be getting old…*
*There's a child in my heart*
*you can see it in my eyes...*
*I didn't see the devil in disguise ...*
*I stand here on the shoreline...*
*Asking only one question: "Which ocean is mine?"*

*"All the oceans are yours Dear Soul...to explore*
*it all depends on you...*
*And what you're searching for?*
*All the oceans are yours...*
*Let the waves embrace your skin and soul kindly...completely...*
*Let each wave penetrate you deeply...*
*Come in to me...*
*Let your rays' sun in to me...deeply...completely"*

*All the jigsaws can be changed...rearranged*

## 27. No Pieces Missing

*There are no pieces missing...*
*All life is complete indeed...*
*All the answers are contained... in every fruit and seed*

*There are no pieces missing...*
*There are no pieces to throw away...*
*Embrace...with grace and gratitude*
*before the whole jigsaw*
*is boxed away...*
*Dear Life....Embrace every jigsaw...with love and compassion*
*Learn to play...*
*All the jigsaws are complete...*

*"It was I....who missed a heartbeat"*

## 28. Debts

*I have never been alone in the morning...*
*the beautiful sunrise...*
*in your gentle breezy eyes...*

*I have never been alone in the afternoon...*
*the summer warm...*
*in the blankets of your arms...*

*I've been lonely half of all my nights*
*and even lonelier half of all my days...*
*Dear Heart...you have erased them all away...*
*Which day is this?*
*I have never seen this kind a night...*
*How do I describe your soul light*

*I have never been alone in the evening...*
*there are songs in the sunset...*
*cancelling all my karmic debts*

## 29. Seasons Brief

Seasons of joy are brief...
Ask any autumn leaf

Seasons of love are small
Ask any lonely heart to reveal it all
and they will say...
No season ever stays...
All seasons go away...

Seasons of quiet are few...
Ask any soul to tell you true
and they will say
noise can make a soul go astray ...
No heart is content alone...
No heart can bear being too long on their own...

Seasons of sharing life are brief
Just when it's about to blossom...one leaves.

Seasons of kind laughter are not many
there are billions of faces lost in a crowd, ask any.
And they will reveal
we have forgotten how to truly feel
Love...joy...quiet...laughter
And the heart only wonders after
all that matters are gone...
and we are on our own...

So embrace all that is dear today...
Hold on...Hold on...tightly...
Don't let go...or they'll all slip away...
some will wither away...
Some will go astray and some just fade away

I know nothing lasts forever but some things come to end too soon
there are some voids in my balloon.
Let me hold you in my eyes and heart and feel it all
In case I too am destined one day... to endure a season of fall

# 30. May I

*May I ask you a question?*
*"Is there any relationship that remains always true?*
*I have been searching a lifetime*
*I wish I knew...."*

*"Yes...All and None...*
*Many ...not even one"*

*I ask many questions*
*for that is the way I am made*
*God used earth of a "questioning" grade*

*How quickly we forget*
*How quickly we forget all our regrets...*
*Many a courageous soldier...many a loving Mother...many a kind wife*
*so easily forgotten...*
*"But that's life"*
*Many a dear friend...many a caring Father and Brother, too*
*the list is long...but it is nothing new.*

*We forget easily and so quickly*
*what we should never forget*
*and remember what we should forget and erase from our lives*
*and they are still with us yet...*

*Some relationships die too quickly*
*I wonder whether they were ever alive*
*some endure the roughest of storm*
*and still survive...*

*Is there anything in this life?*
*That is sacred and true?*
*Let me think ....*
*"Dear Heart....You"*

## 31. Locks & Curls

*Which is more beautiful...Locks and curls*
*or a soul as it unfurls?*
*I got to know...*
*My mind is getting slow...*
*I can't seem to tell which is which...*
*Both feel the same when I kiss...*

*Which is more wonderful...summer skies*
*or your laughing eyes?*
*I got to know...*
*My heart is getting slow...*
*I can't tell the difference anyhow...*
*Both feel the same...Both make me wow...*

*How can I compare...soul and hair*
*skies and eyes...?*
*All I see is beautiful...when my soul flies*
*Is there a way...to define a day...*
*and how something...someone can make you feel*
*when will God reveal?*

*Which is more amazing...a kind embrace*
*or your loving face?*
*I need to know...*
*I know I'm getting slow...*
*I can't tell the difference even when it shows*
*Guess that's how internal beauty flows...*
*Everything beautiful simply glows*
*The morning is not just beautiful but kind, too...*
*Let that beautiful kindness embrace you....Always dear soul*

## 32. 21 grams

*Just what do you lose when you lose it all?*
*How many tons of air?*
*When it's all empty...Just what is left there?*

*Unspoken words...?*
*Unsaid prayer...?*
*When there is nothing there*
*what is there?*

*You have taken away my son...*
*and emptied my plate*
*all the blossoms are gone*
*only desert outside my gate*
*Sands of time*
*have trickled away*
*what is left in what is left in today?*
*I'd rather throw it all away...*

*What does it matter?*
*What's done is done...*
*the war is over...*
*Where is my soldier son?*
*Does it matter to anyone?*

*When we die...What exactly dies?*
*I am searching for truth in an ocean of lies...*
*All soldiers never question the orders...*
*Many have died on foreign borders*
*Dear Life what have you done?*
*The war is over...Please say that you're bringing back my son...*
*Where is my son?*

*I am told when we die...we lose 21 grams in weight...*
*and these 21 grams kill all the blossoms on any family plate*
*and leave a desert by the home gate*
*When I die, you will see*
*The 21 grams was my love for you in me*

### 33. *My Sweet Pea*

*You are the smile on my face*
*the glow in my eye*
*My sweet pea*
*my apple pie*

*You are the rainbow in my life*
*and my summer sun*
*My sweet pea*
*I've only got one…You are the one*

*How lucky can I be ?*
*Life has kindly caressed…I've been blessed… my sweet pea to me*
*Blessings of all blessings*
*God has been kind*
*I've got billions of thoughts*
*But I've got sweet pea on my mind*
*my special one*
*My son*

*You are soft April rain*
*on my meadows and fields*
*Life has many secrets*
*But the secret of all secret has been revealed…*

*Love is all*
*Love is everything*
*My sweet pea*
*is the diamond in my ring*

*Thank you ,Thank you Dear Life*
*what can I say*
*You have made my life*
*a rosary of beautiful days*

## 34. Rain fall…Sun fall

1. I wonder if the rain clouds ever think or feel?
Do they consider the intensity…?
Question the density…of the rainfall before the rainfall?

Do they weigh up and choose…
How much rain is whose…How much rainfall to lose?

Would they vary the width of the pores…?
Is the rainfall more gentle falling on the baby duckling and daffodils?
Is it more intense on parched grassland …
And briefer on the rich green meadows?

Would the grey be kind on me…knowing I have no umbrella
or a tree close by for shelter?

If the rain clouds can think or feel, why are they taking so long to decide
where I stand?

2. The sun came out with shy on its face…
knowing that I am totally drenched and far from home…
Am I going to be subjected to the same intensity…or density sun fall?
I hope both my shirt and my hair dry quickly…
I will look a fool…
leaving home without an umbrella…
after being warned that the weather was subject to change.
And so it is with Life….All Seasons pass…

3. It makes no difference…rain fall or sun fall
both are mindless…unbiased…
They rain and shine on every one…
There are no qualifying conditions…

I think I'll stay here and soak my soul in the sun fall…
and dry a little of the rain fall in my heart

## 35. Relationships

*Would you let me be the trunk or the leaf...?*
*The attachment of one to the other...*
*pure relationship...*
*No weight...*
*Pure essence of love*

*We all complain...I am no exception...*
*sometimes the shoulders simply...*
*need to pause and rest...*
*and regain direction and perspective*

*And we all lose something along the way...*
*something that is good and cherished...*
*but tired shoulders can utter words in haste....*
*and we have had those moments...*
*uttering words in haste...*

*Can I make the water flow back under the bridge?*
*How can I take this moment back to yesterday....?*
*There is only one way...*
*Only one road that will take me back to where I want to be...*
*"Dear Heart...Find the humility to admit and courage to*
*accept...when you are to know that you are wrong...*

*And it takes a strong man to say...*
*I am sorry and I stand before you naked...forgive me...*
*punish me...Let me learn I have been wrong..."*

*What can I say?*
*I feel lighter now that I've got my pride and ego out of the way*

## 36. Home

I've been lost before
I know what it's all about...
Life has been kind with its teaching
I now know without shadow of a doubt...

Find love and you find purpose
Give love and you've said a prayer
Dear life thank you for caring
Dear Life thank you for teaching me the principles of care
"Be where you are supposed to be... Be close...Be closer...Be there"

I've been lonely, too
No heart is spared or exempt
Love has been kind with its forgiveness
I now know what you meant

Find love and you find meaning
Meaning is what we are meant to find
Dear love thank you for the library in your kind eyes
"Be a candle for a searching mind...most of us are blind"

I've know what lonely can be
I know what it can do...
But I have learnt Dear Life
What I know now...but how I wish I knew
then...Some roads and maps have many lonely bends...
there is only one road to be on when a heart is alone...Home...Sweet Home

I know some roads are meant to be travelled alone
When I am on these roads and alone
Dear Life...Remind me all roads can take you home...take me home

## 37. Spin the Ball

There is nothing like a soul
totally exposed and bare
I believe God plants
abundance there...

Seasons of plenty
Season with more
Seasons of kind blessings
Seasons that grow behind open doors...

Dear Soul open up...open the door
And share Seasons of true abundance
once again...once more
I'm not sure what I've lost
Not sure what I'm searching for...
Lot of water has gone under the bridge
Whatever it is that I need, it has yet to knock on my door

I'm not sure where or when
Not sure why
Lot of summers have come and gone
Which one left the winter in my eye ?
Who?
What?
When?
Did the winters enter my eye?
Why?

I've been full all my life
Life has been kind with its fill...
Which moment turned to stone?
Which diamond left behind its autumn chill?
Some diamonds always do...and always will

I'm not sure how the early morning
some times weigh heavy on the soul and the shoulders
All of a sudden
You feel feeble and a million years older
Which heart beat left the soul and the skin so many years older?

Some nights I empty out all the closets
hoping that I'll find
Some where in the bin
my mind
Lately most of the nights have not been that kind
I don't hold it against the moment
I don't really mind

I'm not sure what I've lost
I 'm not sure at all
It is what it is
Dear Life spin the ball
I'm all in
It's one of those days
I'll either rise like a phoenix or fall...I've made my bets, spin the ball...

## 38. Questions

The hardest question for many
is how to face the day
only a few live it...most will waste it away...
and it's one of those days...
When a searching heart can go astray...

Dear Life you have filled me
You have been generous and kind
Some nights have left empty spaces...
and numbed my skin and mind...
and left me behind...
struggling with questions
Where? When? Why?
We have shared so many summers...
who left the winters in my eye?
I hope I find out before the skin and soul dies
I woke up early...both heavy headed and angry
knowing that the only thing I can change for sure...
in my lifetime...is me.

I have tried in vain to change the world...

I now accept my mission in life...
make the change in myself that I would like to see in others

I have wasted so much time...so much sand
has drained away from my timer...

Why do I still doubt and question how real change happens?

Fool ...wake up if you want any dreams to come true...

Every heart must chisel the stone ...and along the
way endure periods of drought and desert...

Let the heart stay fertile always...

Make the change today....
not to surrender ever...
even when the odds are against you and the moment has long gone...

I woke up early...and angry...but now I am calm and understanding...
I have changed

<u>An Afterthought</u>
Never falling out are what good decisions are all about

## 39. Kind Seasons

*We are all blossoms from a kind season...*
*which had its reasons*
*to be kind...*
*We are all an expression of a generous mind...*

*Seasons come...Seasons go*
*that's how the rosary of moments flows...*
*Where it all comes from...or where it all goes when it goes...*
*Who knows?*
*I know no one knows...*

*Some seasons are gentle on the soul and skin*
*they warm the heart...and the skin...*

*Some seasons remain detached...*
*How brutal they can be...cannot be matched*

*I know how I cried...the day my Mother died...*
*One breath we were holding hands...*
*and the next I lost her in the sands...*

*Time is a little like the wine...*
*Some vineyards leave sadness...*
*and some barrels hold the finest of the fine...*
*We must learn to sip both...when we dine...*
*both are a blessing in their own way*
*I never throw any away...*
*I sip both with gratitude when I sip mine...*

*Oh...how I cried...the day my father died...*
*One breath he was walking with his soulful son...*
*the next breath, it was all done*

*Some seasons become kinder by the day*
*they make you believe they will always stay...*
*and then you greet the final day*
*when it's all taken away...*
*and you stand...looking up towards the sky...*
*Not sure if any one hears your heart whispering:" Why...Dear Life why?"*

*Oh how I cried...the day love died...*

*Some seasons bring only questions...*
*leaving even more questions in reply...*
*the hardest of all seasons...*
*is when someone...something dies...*
*How do you face that moment...?*
*How do you cope?*
*When life opens your fingers*
*and you have to let go of the rope?*

*I have found that God was kind*
*when he left billions of questions in my mind.*
*All seasons are what they are*
*some were created to balm the soul*
*and some to leave scars...*
*Both seasons have their role to play*
*and my soul must embrace them both today...*

*Oh how I cried...when what was meant for sharing was subjected to divide*

*Seasons come ...seasons go*
*that's how the moments flow*

*Seasons go...seasons come*
*only some understand the sum*

# 40. Crossroads

*I came to the crossroads with arms open wide...*
*"Dear Crossroad ...You decide...which road I should take...*
*Which ties I should strengthen and which ones I should untie and break...*
*Dear Life...Help me so that I make no mistake"*

*I came with my retiring body but an open mind...*
*Some of candles lit the road...and some were like flares...left me blind...*
*Why are the candles sometimes both kind and unkind?*
*If I am on the wrong road...How will I find what I need to find?"*

*Some lives are ruled purely by greed*
*and some by need...*
*Why do you seek to add more...?*
*God has left so many kind thoughts and gestures by your door...*
*And yet you are still hungry...*
*I'm not sure...are you sure?*

*I came to resolve and dissolve or take away*
*I came here today to leave more than, I, perhaps*
*in moments of blindness took away*
*I will not stay...*
*But I leave you my love for always*
*should you ever regain your old self ...and become sane again...*
*Call me my dear life...my dear friend...*
*May the purpose of life enter your soul...*
*and make you whole…*
*It breaks my heart...to see you losing your pure colours in the devils art*

## 41. Traveller

*I have travelled on a million buses and trains*
*not much remains*
*to see*
*the buses and trains were kind*
*on my aimless soul*
*and me...*

*I have travelled on a million boats and planes*
*not much remains*
*to see*
*the boats and planes were kind*
*on my roaming heart*
*and me*

*I never found it where I was*
*haven't found it where I'm at*
*some trains took me to tomorrow*
*some buses brought me back...*
*some planes took me forward*
*some boats took me back...*
*and I am dearly searching...for something I still clearly lack*

*I have searched a million oceans and seas*
*not many remain*
*Not one left their tie on me...I can hardly remember their names...*
*Life's been kind at million crossroads*
*they all lead me to you*

*I've been friends with a million hearts and souls*
*but none of them will do*
*I was searching for you...I am searching for you*

## 42. New Start

Let the New day start
with optimism and courage in the heart...
fearless and totally free
from any thoughts that held back "me" reaching the true potential in "me"

Let the New Year roll
with fresh yearning for learning in the soul
spirit soaring
Trying to seize all that is beautiful in any moment
And get more in...
Let the New Year begin

## 43. Leave a Candle

Leave a candle in the porch...
I'm coming home tonight...
A man can get lost in the night
and it's that kind a night....

Leave a kiss on every crossroad...
and let it show me the way...
A man can take the wrong turning...
and it's that kind a day...

I've been travelling a long time
I've been lost that long....
I've made lot of right decisions
that were clearly wrong...
I need to get it right
before this day is thru'
I thought I knew
what I clearly never knew...
What should I do?
Who should I turn to?

Leave a heart beat near my heart
teach me what I need to learn...
I have missed many a turn...
Let me take another turn...

I could easily fall apart....
I could easily lose my way...
A man can miss a shinning sign
And it's that kind a day

God leave me a star on every crossroad
and some needle and thread on every bridge
I have burnt many a safe crossing
and this is that kind a ridge

Leave some starlight in my soul
and some stars in my eyes
A soul can die on any highway
and it's one of those highways where a soul often dies

## 44. Beautiful Reason

*Wishing you warm regards*
*and kind blessings*
*Beautiful Season…*

*Wishing you kind regards*
*and heart's caressing*
*Beautiful Season….A Beautiful Reason*

*Open your heart and pour out…love*
*give some away….*
*It's a beautiful day…to give some away…*

*I wish I'd done it long a go …*
*I wish I knew then what I now know…*
*Give it all away…*
*It's a beautiful day….*

*Open up your arms and let love walk in…*
*Let the beautiful season begin…*
*Goodwill …sharing…soul to soul caring*

*When was the last time you opened up your arms*
*and opened up your heart…*
*"Never…Never…Never"*
*"It's a beautiful day to start….A beautiful*
*season…a beautiful reason to start"*

## 45. Larry Crowne

Left school early and moved on
was a cook in the Navy...twenty years gone...?
One day... Like an old shoe thrown away...
Larry Crowne...going down

Joined evening classes to learn
just when I messed up my turn....
One day I was here...the next day gone...
Bluntly reminded it was time to move on....
Larry Crowne...gone

You changed it all...I'm so glad that I found you...
I want to build my new world around you...
One thing that is clear...I am happy that you're here
Larry Crowne...finally found

# 46. Roots

"Dear Life, find me"
There is a reason to be found
I've been wanting to fly...
on the soul in my eye...
But there are stronger reasons on the ground....

Who could that person be....embracing my soul...grounding me?
Dear Heart ...sail and fly ... the waterfalls in my eye

I've been running since the moment I was born
been running ever since
Need to slow down
grow some roots in to the ground
Before the soil begins to mince...

Who could that person be....embracing my heart...grounding me?
Dear Soul ...sail and fly ... the waterfalls in my eye

Embrace me in your eyes...
Dear Life...Kind me
kindly lay the maps in my soul
Dear Life...find me
I've been coming home since the day I was born
I've always had the key.
How could I find something not lost...?
Or something that hasn't cost
I only lost myself somewhere in me....
But I am found....got the roots back in the ground
I've shared so many summers
there are rainbows in my heart
Let me be your starburst
when I fall apart...

## 47. Umbrella's in my Heart

*I saw her struggling...almost giving in under the rainfall...*
*Some drops can be too heavy on an ageing heart...*
*And I have seen a few, fall apart...*

*She carries on walking...hoping that some passing cloud may show kindness*
*and let a few rays of sunshine thru'*
*the sun was trying...But I'm not sure the clouds knew*
*I just supposed they do...*

*Some clouds can be merciless...*
*not caring if any flower beds come apart...*
*or some weakly attached petals wash away...*
*or some ageing soul comes apart...and implode the heart*

*Some eyes know how to hold back the strain and the tears...*
*She has done that for so many years...*
*But today is a different kind a day...*
*I saw a tear slip away...*
*She wiped her eyes and wiped her soul...*
*Today of all days...She must remain intact... and whole...*

*Some clouds wash*
*and some clouds drain*
*some clouds leave no trace*
*and some all the fragmented remains...*
*Some clouds soothe*
*and some clouds drown*
*some take away the jokers*
*and some bring the clowns...*
*I have played many roles*
*but I have yet to act the part...*

*"Dear Life let me share the umbrella's in my heart*

*If I must share anything, let me share today...*
*Before her ageing heart slips away"*

## 48. Simple Man

Am I a storm...?
Do I warm...or do I excel in harm?
Tearing down boats and sails...
with rain and wind that lashes and impales...
Am I kind in my intentions or have I been a heartless nail?

I hope I am warming
truly pray I'm not harming
in my intentions or ways...
what is your judgement...?
What do you say?

Am I worthy of keeping?
Or am I best thrown away?
What do you say?

I say if you must walk away...
let me embrace you one more time...
I thought you knew me...

The nails are not mine...
they were fired at you by the world...
I tried to shield you
but they went thru' me...

My skin is all bruises and holes...
and so is my heart and soul

I hope that I warm you
It is not me who's trying to harm you
I am a simple man...I don't lie
I have always lived for you...and so it will be when I die

# 49. Dare

I dare you, to bare...
and expose your core
I have seen your skin...
I want to see who lies within...
I want to know more...

How deep and wide...You are inside...?
Are you shallow...or deep and rich?
Tell me...Which?

I have seen so many souls in camouflage
hiding behind walls
I would not know who they are
until the mask falls...
Life is to short anyhow
why make it even harder to see?
Dear Life remove all camouflage from me.

I do not want to hide...
I want expose it all...so the world can see ...the real me...from deep inside

Like a caterpillar waiting at the edge of a leaf...
Waiting for some kind butterfly to fly by and add wings to the belief
stirring ...."Can I fly?"
"Well, Dear Heart....not unless you try"

It is only when we lose our mask
we ask,
the right questions with our heart
until then life is just a false start

## 50. Wild Flower

I wish there was someone out there
who truly cares to be, honest with honesty...
We all lie...that's how most of live and die...
Believing...self-deceiving...

I am a wave
searching in the sea,
for the missing part of me...

The sea can be soothing
loneliness removing...
kind and embracing
and help in retracing
all that's lost or gone...
How all the waves...like life...keep moving on?

Like a wildflower growing in a quiet corner
on a mountain side...
parched and waiting on rain
or a gentle tide...
aching to be...
closer to some gentle breeze
wishing but not sure what it's missing
but knowing
the loneliness or the aloneness of growing
in a quiet corner on a mountain side
waiting on the rain on the harsh side of the plain

*I wish there was someone out there*
*who truthfully cares?*
*A wildflower waiting on answers:*
*"What is my destiny....Take me there… All else will only bring disrepair?"*

*Like a river flowing through a forest*
*lost among the shrubs and trees…*
*asking only one question:*
*"Which way is home dear breeze?"*
*"Home is where the heart is…*
*close your eyes and flow…*
*Which way is home?*
*Your soul knows…*
*Follow the voice in your head…*
*listen to what's been said…*
*Slow down and you will see*
*the details…to your destiny"*

*I know there is some one out there*
*who cares*
*"Dear Life…let me flow and go…where I'm meant to be"*

## 51. Heart

I have sent you my love
in my heart...
take care how you take the wrapping apart...
You just might
throw away a few heart beats from my heart...

Have you ever taken a flower apart?
Petal by petal...
to the centre of its essence
the flowers heart...

Did you know that all flowers have a heart?
They only expose it to those
who love the rose
and the way even God
closes his eyes
when the rose shares its fragrance
with the summer skies.

I am not sure whether I am a flower or the garden?
All I know is that I seek Life's pardon
for rushing by...
the summer fragrance in the summer skies.

If I stay long enough in prayer
Will God meet me there?
Like the fragrance ...
reaching out for the summer air

Take away the wrapping with care...
Somewhere inside my heart is there
for you...with fragrance new
Unwrap me...take me apart but never swap me

## 52. Detail

*I have missed so much detail in my life...*
*I often wonder why I sleep thru' long train journeys...*
*I should gaze and amaze my eye...*
*Dear Life I've been sleep travelling too long...*

*Wake me...Wake me before this short life passes*
*me by untasted by my eye and soul*

*Dear Life take away all sleep from my eyes and let me not miss a thing...*
*anymore...I have missed too much already*

*For the first time I can feel the warmth in every breath...*
*misting up the window and my eyes at the same time...*

## 53. Misty Eyed

*Too tired to stay awake...too weary to kneel and pray...*
*I thought I got away with it...not saying my prayers for a day or two.*

*Watching you sleeping I suddenly felt urgency to kneel and pray...*
*Seeing the innocence on your face...untouched...undiluted...pure...*
*how vulnerable you look...*
*Oh. How will you survive...it's a rough World out there.*

*Every heart running fast... too fast to even know*
*what they'll miss by travelling too fast....*

*I want to pause long enough to say a quiet prayer...while you sleep*
*asking...begging protection and warm blankets for your heart always...*

*Dear Life take my blankets if you are ever in short supply....*
*But let not this totally unaware soul ever face the storm or winter alone....*

## 54. Inside

*Rattle it to see*
*what rocks inside of me*

*Shake it to see*
*what rattles inside of me*

*Check every breath*
*Check every heart beat*
*Check my soul*
*Check under every sheet*
*The man that I am…is there somewhere*
*Don't lose your patience...find me*
*I am loose sheets of life*
*Dear Life bind me...*

*Stir my heart to see*
*which heart beats, beat in me*

*Scoop my soul to see*
*the quality of the soul in me.*

*If you find nothing there*
*and if all you find is barren and bare*
*Dear Heart have mercy on my life*
*and leave a prayer there*

*Rattle it to see*
*what rolls inside of me.*

*Shake me to see*
*which bubbles are still grounded in me....*
*Release me, let me fly*
*on rich heart beats in my eye*

*Can you see*
*the soul in me?*
*It's all in my eyes...*
*Look totally naked....no disguise*

*Dear Life, Rattle and Roll*
*Leave some music in my soul*

*An Afterthought*
*Dear Life you have filled me with an attitude... of pure gratitude*

## 55. Seen you in the Sun

*I have seen you in the sun...*
*I want to see you in the night...*
*When the night is done*
*I want to sleep in your soul light*

*I have seen you in the night*
*Like a lighthouse you are a constant light*
*For lost souls in life's sea*
*Your lighthouse saved me…*

*Now I want to see you in the day*
*To light the clouds away*
*I have seen you in the day*
*And how you night the day away…*

*Sunshine warm eyes and skin*
*How you warm my soul within…*
*Now I want to see you in the night…*
*And share the starlight*
*In your soul*
*And light up my nights of charcoal…*
*Mine me till you find*
*The diamonds misplaced by life in my heart and mind.*

*I got fragrance in my soul…*
*Searching for the springtime breeze…*
*I have been lost on these meadows…*
*"Which way is your heart light, please?"*

I must find the lost flowers
My garden is empty and bare...
I have misplaced the bible in my heart...
And I have lost all my prayers...

Can you hear me?
Are you anywhere near me?
Guide me... Light some maps deep inside me...
Let me Captain the sea... and find me.

Like the butterfly not sure
Darting from flower to flower...
But this is not the time to be lost...
After all this is my finest hour...

Let me calibrate the compass...
Let me reset the sails...
Send Judas back on his way...
And hand him back all his nails...

There are maps in my soul
There are maps in my eyes...
There are oceans in my heart...
My soul holds the maps of the universe and its skies...

Close my eyes... and slowly breathe...
There is relationship between each heart beat...
No weight... just gratitude
How each breath is a life complete...?
There are bibles unread in my eyes
And my soul wants to pray...
My heart's exposing all the pages...
Beating: "Read it all today... before the prayers fade away
Back in to space and time...
And all the bibles in your eyes are no longer just mine"

*Let me close my eyes and kneel*
*Embrace God and experience how it feels...*
*My heart yearns to be*
*A heartbeat from life's harmony...*

*I can never explain why...*
*Life has left so many prayers in my eye...*
*It seems so unfair... But God has left many spares...*
*Until now I never knew...*
*God and Life have both been listening to you ...*
*And heard all your prayers...*
*"Dear God... always be there..."*

*My songbook holds many songs...*
*Nourished by life and beautiful dawns...*
*How can that be?*
*God abundantly blessing me*

*I have seen you in the day...*
*I want to see you in the night...*
*The morning is a long, long time away...*
*I need to share your soul light...*
*A man can get lost in the midnight...*
*Midnights can be dark as a mine of coal*
*The morning sometimes never gets to greet*
*Midnight lost souls...*

*I have seen you in the day*
*Let me share you in the night...*
*There are crossroads in every breath...*
*Let me share your heart light...*

## 56. Empty Handed

*Empty handed we all come*
*Empty handed we all came*
*that's life*
*Yes, that's the game...*

*The interlude...is our opportunity to fill the silence and solitude*
*with love and its warm caressing...*
*and experience some soul dressing ...*

*How do you live with the alone...?*
*Being on your own...?*
*No one home...?*

*How do you learn to deal with the losses*
*and bear all the disappointments and crosses*
*on our shoulders...?*
*Some heavier than mountains and boulders...*
*How do you learn to warm your heart...when it is all getting colder?*

*"Journey in....deep within...*
*that's where you need to be: to find me"*

## 57. Returns

There are prayers
flowing in my eyes...
honey sweet buds from early April...
sharing their fragrance there

There are kind wishes
growing in the orchard of my soul...
sapphire waterfalls...
wanting to make every shore and bank feel whole

Let the oceans flow to the deserts thirsty...
and kindness to the heart hungry for warm and true...
Why am I always flowing towards you?

It's a blessing to receive kindness
and a greater blessing to be kind…
Some souls stay in church all their lives...
Some carry prayers in their mind...
I know which prayers are easier to find
but both bring light...to any kind a night…

There are valleys full of lilacs
in all my dreams...
Can I share some fragrance from my meadows
and seal some of the broken petals in some of your life's seams?

What good is a heart and all its heartbeats if
it can't share love and forgive...?
I may be alive and breathing...
But have I learnt to live?
Have I learnt to share and give...?
Have I learnt to forgive?
Let me spend this season…and learn all I need to learn
About sharing and returns

## 58. The Priest

*The Priest worried and worries still for my fast ageing soul...*
*saying that I was getting too close to God...and too far from life*
*and if I did and do...*
*what purpose will I serve...here...*

*Hardly anyone was here last Sunday...*
*Except those seeking ...or lost within them...*

*What he doesn't know is that I am getting closer to God*
*only because I am no longer lost ...or seeking*
*and as for the purpose...*
*I thought we were all born...to know God...*
*and make the journey...*
*closing the distance...*
*I feel God is only a breath away...*
*He is the next breath I'll take...and what makes my heart continue to beat*

## 59. Come share my Fragile

Come share my fragile with me...
I am...I am...and I need to be...just be

How fragile my skin...
You can almost see the soul within...

How fragile the seams...
You can almost see all my dreams...

We are all fragile seeking the threads...
that we can tie
and make our dreams fly ...
and fly I do...
When I share my fragile with you

How fragile the skin...
and how enduring the soul within
Come share my sky
When I fly

## 60. Without Reserve

*Have I thanked you?*
*I mean thanked you without reserve...*
*My thank you comes from the heart...What you hear is sincere*

*Sometimes a heart can live a lifetime and never pause long enough*
*to realise what...who...Kept it beating*
*Thank you for the heart beats...*
*mine and yours...together...*
*I have my own private orchestra here...*
*God is kind...*

## 61. I have thrown away

I have learnt a valuable lesson today
knowing what to throw
what not to throw away

Some people throw out the baby with the water

I have seen many a heart...torn apart
from the deleting and the purging
the sorting and the merging
Can't see the wood from the trees...

And all the love once here...sent to the slaughter

We all clear out baggage at some moment in our life
I've had my clearing days...
Things dear to me
I have thrown some of them away
Dear Life remind me...How to track back and find me

# 62. Significance

I used to get wiser as I got older...
Nowadays I just seem to age...
adding no more to my heart or soul.

I seem to have got lost somewhere
among finding myself
and knowing who I am...

I am like the sun which seeks qualification
before it shares its sunrays with pale skin...
What type of snare am I caught in?

Does the mind resort to self-importance
when it is empty or when it's full?

I seem to forget how important we are is not measured by our own eye
but by others...on how important we become in their lives and days...

There is no one I seem to remember whose life or days I have
touched and changed with warmth and kindness...

I should not feel self-importance at all...
I am as important as a cold breeze in season of fall...
Or the rainfall that adds only a sip to the ocean
I am running my day on wrong emotion
I am not important at all
in an ocean I am just a drop of rainfall...

However, if I touch some ones life or day
Significance....more importantly honour may enter the play...
and change all my days.

I must learn soon how to be wise
which is of more value: significance or self importance in the eyes?

<u>An Afterthought</u>
The whole purpose of my life...is to mine...
the join between my soul and the divine

## 63. Almost

*We are almost there...the new day is almost here*
*a few more heart beats...*
*Share with me the early spring in your breath....*
*Breathe softly on my eyelids...your warm prayers*
*I want to see you and only your face when I open my eyes*

*Today I realise God has been unkind to Slim...*
*undersupplied in love... plentiful of something missing in him...*
*I wonder if he ever wakes up early and see what's missing?*

*Don't let me distract you...*
*I am also like the rest...in need...waiting...hoping....*
*Your breaths change all the storms in my life...*
*I can feel the sun on my skin...or is that your naked heart on my soul?*

## 64. Canto Libri

I close me eyes and I hear a song
whispering "this is the day to start shinning
there are millions of un-mined souls
this is the day to start mining"

Many mines are left untouched
they crumble and die waiting
diamonds and pearls left un-ringed
with some rings long time anticipating...

Know me... Expose me and show me... Reveal me... Let your feelings feel me

My heart is a book of songs...
and my soul a guitar strumming
My soul can hear every heart beat
whispering: "wait for me I am coming
I am just around the bend...
not far behind you
No matter how far away
My compass will find you"

Know me... Expose me and show me... Reveal me... Let your feelings feel me

Every life has its own song
and each page has a different meaning
some words embrace you soft and warm
some come at you like the guitar screaming.

Know me... Expose me and show me... Reveal me... Let your feelings feel me

One day when all this is over
and all my rosary's of life are finally broken
Not a heart will spare a breath
and the joker stops all his joking
I am just around the bend...
not far behind you
No matter how far away
My heart will still find you

## 65. Fusion

*Do you cry when something or someone dies?*
*Will you cry?*
*When I breathe my final breath and die?*

*When the winter claims the summered leaf?*
*Does the tree now naked and bare... show grief?*
*When a blade of grass withers and die*
*Do the meadows cry?*

*Do the oceans cry....?*
*When life that lives within it dies?*

*I think we all experience loss....*
*and we all bear the cross...*
*of sadness and grief...*
*for every blade of grass and every autumn leaf...*

*How does the heart...start the first heartbeat?*
*What makes the seed grow...?*
*Dear Life...I want to know...*
*I am learning...Let me explore*
*and find some of the answers on these shores...*

*How do we think?*
*All my dreams and thoughts...Just who holds all the links?*
*I want to know...*
*Dear Life will you expose your hand...and show*
*I am a student...there is yearning in my heart and soul*
*I need to know...What part I am, am I of the whole?*

*Love is more than the union of physical parts*
*It is more a fusion of the souls*
*and oneness of the hearts*
*I do not want just an illusion*
*I want to be part of a perfect fusion*

## 66. Rescore me

Everything has changed
The score's been rearranged
The music has estranged
Take this rich semibreve
Look how it misses and grieves
You are leaving....

Take these lonely quavers
See how the heart and soul wavers
You are leaving...
And these whispering crochets, pauses and rests
Was the music at its best...?
And the soulful, wistful minims
Have so much soul still in 'em
Now quietly sighing...slowly dying
You are leaving...

The music needs playing...
That's what the silence is saying...
Play me...rescore me...need me ...crave me
Take these lost notes from the stave and re-stave me....
There's so much music in my heart
Needing rhythm and rhyming ...
It seems I have lost my time
I need fresh timing....

Take these lonely notes...
And embrace me...
I am lost in space...
Rearrange and re-space me
Take these lonely minims...Fill your music in 'em
And the pauses and rests...Hold them close to your chest...
Hear the heart beats...pure and neat...perfectly complete

## 67. The Rye in my Eye

It's been one of those evenings
one of those night...
When what has always been right doesn't feel right...
It's that kind a night

I'm not looking for answers
there are no questions on my mind...
Its one of those nights
when I'll take what ever I may find
got vineyards in my veins...
and waterfalls in my eye...
Tonight the waterfall needs a dye...so pour me some rye
I'm tired of waiting waterfalls
I need some rye in my eye...

It's been one of those seasons
with snow and rain...
When what has always been wrong doesn't feel wrong...
that seasons back again

I'm not asking any questions
I see it crystal clear...
I've had my share of the wine
Now I need some rye here
Got vineyards in my heart
embracing every heartbeat
Tonight my soul needs a dye...so pour me some rye
I'm tired of waiting waterfalls
I need some rye for my eye...

*Pour it slow and long*
*Till I say enough...*
*throw in some ice*
*I want to sip it neat and rough*

*Let me close my eyes*
*and enjoy the night*
*the rye in my eye*
*shinning in starlight*

*I got no time to waste*
*I've wasted enough*
*Let me learn to live*
*I'm missing out on that stuff*
*Got tomorrow in my heart*
*And I'm not looking back*
*I've been going around in circles*
*on a one way track*
*Tonight the clocks asking why?...to the waterfall in my eye*
*I need to learn to fly....without the rye in my eye*

## 68. The Rust in my Heart

I am the best at passing time
sipping wine...
I have done that all my days...
I look back...
and walk some of those familiar tracks
my how my time has ticked away

I am good at lot of things...
A craftsman...the Boss
One thing I find hard to deal with is loss...

I lost my Father long ago...
I can still recall ...
some things blurring...some things crystal clear
the final day my Father was here...
How I cried that day...
When in his sleep he slipped away...
And I still fall apart
From the fatigue and rust in my heart...

I lost my Mom...
some five years ago...
that morn...I woke up at dawn ... sitting by her bed that day
had her hand in my hand when she went away
to where ever we go when we go
I cried all night wanting to know...
whether the final breath knows
Where it all goes
While laying in my bed I came apart
From the missing and the yearning in my heart

I can deal with most things in life
one thing weighs heavy on my cross
I find it hard to deal with loss
I lost my brother somewhere
and he knew his way
But I lost him that day
and he never came back...such is the darkness on some tracks
and high ways they never bring you home
But only take you away
I held his picture in my hand and I cried and cried
What dies when it all dies inside?
The whole world saw me come apart
From the fatigue and the rust in my heart
I don't seem to plan anymore
I don't seem to care
I find it hard to deal with loss
for years the morning breeze combed my hair...

I look back and I see
my family and me...
not much remains...
Where is the consolation to keep my ageing mind sane
you are still here
among the laughter and tears...?
What is, is and that's all there is
Why am I slow to learn
the purpose of a flame is to burn...
and not come apart
From the fatigue in my body and the rust in the heart

## 69. Handkerchief

With a small tear in her eye and a trembling voice, she said:
"We need to talk...Come let us walk ...
I feel I have been disrespected...
Something that I never expected...
I haven't slept at all ...
You left me in a freefall..."

"Just what did I do or say...to make you feel that way?"

"You did not say...what you should've said...
And that has left a vacuum and numbness in my head...
You didn't do what you should've done...
But you can still do the undone...
and apologise...For the tears in my eyes...
I feel disrespected...
Something I never expected..."

"Dear Friend I apologise...If I left any tears in your eyes...
I have always meant well...
I was hoping you could tell...
I am always on your side...
Let my heart handkerchief your tear swept eyes

# 70. Tall Men

*Do tall men fall first...?*

*We all walk as if packing steel RSJ's in our shoulders and backbone ...*

*But who will today open up and declare:*

*"I am fragile like you....seeking strength in the usual places...usual faces"*

*We all carry monkeys on our shoulders...only a
few ever truly manage to lose them...
or solve them totally...*

*I openly declare:
"I am trying to resolve all the monkeys on my shoulders...
and I declare I may not solve then all"*

*I am a tall man...but I am fragile just like you*

## 71. The Chair

You have a chair
The world needs to see
This is the chair
Where you shared your soul with me…

The chair has aged with time and flow
But still character it retains
This is where we sipped our wine
And shared our smiles and pain…

This is the very chair
Where I opened up my heart
And you with your kind eyes
Put together all the separate parts…

You took each heart beats and embraced them in to a rosary
That's when I learnt how kind, kindness can be

I found all the lost reasons
And the misplaced rhymes
This is where we shared all our vineyards
And the stocks of our finest wines…

This is the chair where you exposed your soul
To my searching soul
This is the very chair where I found my life
And became whole…
Don't ever give away or throw our darling chair
This is where I found heaven…my god lives there

## 72. The Darling Chair

*Pull up close to hear*
*there are waterfalls in my heartbeats*
*there are heartbeats in this tear...*

*You've been abandoned*
*and left to dust and decay*
*is this how our heartbeats*
*ebb away...?*

*Time is friends with no one*
*the Seasons come and go*
*even the strongest of foundation*
*withers and weaken when the cold seasons blow...*
*Which brick they split open and why*
*only the brick knows…?*

*The foundations and the walls*
*are all slowly coming apart*
*as are the ageing heartbeats*
*and the ageing heart...*

*Dear chair...I should've kept you*
*wrapped in cotton wool and soul*
*the seasons have been unkind*
*and the unkind seasons take their toll...*

Let me heal away the splinters
and feel away the tears
let me share your deserts and the meadows
and plant some blossoms there...

You have shared your Bible
and all your prayer
and it is time
that I repaid my debts there ...and repair the disrepair

Heal away...
Feel away...
Heart to Heart...Soul to Soul
Life is a rosary of fragments
but we have always made each other feel whole...
Feel away...
I'm all in, deal away...

Darling chair...it is crystal clear...
You are here because you're meant to be here...
You and me...each others Destiny
God was generous and kind
When he left you in my mind

## 73. Come There

*Captain Sunshine*
*Come and rest inside my soul*
*in the sun there*
*and the sunshine in my prayer...*
*Come there...*

*Captain Starlight*
*Come and sleep inside my heart*
*in the stars there*
*and the starlight in my prayer...*
*Come there...*

*We are all seekers...searching for something*
*only few will ever find*
*and the rest will roam with restless minds...*
*Come home and be kind*
*to this searching heart...*
*before the autumn winters it apart...*
*Come save this heart*

*Captain Moonlight*
*Come and shine on my ageing skin*
*in the life there*
*and the light in my prayer...*
*Come there...*

*We are all travellers...searching for homes*
*only few will ever find*
*Captain Soul light not many souls are kind...*
*Please be kind...*
*Come easy on my mind...*
*I'll wait there...*
*with all my prayers...*
*to wish your soul always...beautiful days*

## 74. Fire

*Dear Heart, I seek fire*
*Where is the sun...the one?*

*I seek the ocean...*
*Where all the waves are motions of devotion*

*I seek the meadows and valleys and the mountain sides*
*where my heart can explore*
*forevermore.*

*How long do you wish to stay...?*
*Dear Heart, heartbeat the magic words...For Always*

*let me explore this shore and find forevermore*

## 75. Me & the Fox

*We had a special relationship,*
*me and the fox.*
*She always thought I never knew*
*But I always knew that I knew.*

*She was a little like the lonely squirrel*
*in late September...*
*hoarding, gathering*
*selfishly storing*
*ignoring all others*
*interested only in self and self preservation.*

*I wonder if she ever realised*
*there are others, too*
*hungry, waiting, and patient.*

*Such is the call of an empty belly or any threats*
*of an empty rumbling belly.*

*The winter is fast approaching.*
*All the leaves are dead and crisp dry.*
*This morning there is something winter in my eye.*

*I have a few spare pine nuts*
*should I offer them to her or better still hide them under a leaf*
*so she can find them easily...*
*I know she does not accept charity or kind gestures...*
*But I would not want her to experience a hungry day...*
*I think I'll give all my reserves away...*
*It is a special kind a day*
*I wouldn't want the winter to take all my summer thoughts away.*

*I don't care if I know, what she thinks, I don't know*
*Today, I just want the day to flow*

## 76. The Secret

*I have seen beautiful in you*
*Beautiful I never knew...*
*before*
*See, what I can see*
*now that you have opened your door....*

*Hide not behind masks...walls ...closed doors...*
*True barriers for sure...*
*I want to know*
*what fertilises your beautiful soul*
*and how it grows....*
*Through seasons kind and unkind*
*I want to see the sun in your mind...*

*I too want to find*
*the roads to travel*
*when the seasons are kind and unkind...*
*What rivers to cross*
*and which ones to leave alone*
*which bridges to share*
*and which ones to cross on my own...*

*The secret is stay fresh*
*Gently breeze seasons of famine and less ...*

*There is nothing like a soul*
*totally exposed and bare*
*I believe God plants*
*abundance there...*

*Seasons of plenty*
*Season with more*
*Seasons of kind blessings*
*Seasons that grow behind open doors...*

*Dear Soul open up...open the door*
*And share Seasons of true abundance*
*once again...once more*

## 77. Missed

*Dear life I have missed you....*
*Guess I love you so*
*you are like a river*
*kind to everything in its flow*

# 78. Look Up

*You got to have the sky*
*in your eyes*
*to fly....*

*Dear Heart learn to fly*
*There are rainbows waiting in the sky*
*to colour your eyes*
*and line it rich blue*
*a hue so true*
*A hue meant for you....*

*Learn to always look up*
*and never to long down*
*your roots are deep and strong*
*you honour the ground....*

*Spread your soul and fly...*
*There are rainbows waiting for your eye*

# 79. Till Then

*You ask me: "When?"*
*I replied: "You must wait till then"*

*We are eager to fill our pockets*
*all chasing the same gentle breeze...*
*All looking after number one*
*Long forgotten how to say: "Please"*

*We have lost concern*
*for other struggling souls*
*we selfishly guard against*
*sharing any of their tolls*
*How we have learnt to walk away*
*and not even look their way.*

*We no longer care for any one*
*See what looking after number one has done*
*Living in a fortress*
*behind many walls...*
*Making sure we hear no one call...*
*And carry on*
*seeking our wave in the sea*
*Looking after the voice inside your head:*
*"Me and only me"*

*You ask me: "When"*

*I say: "Each road has its own bends*
*each journey its own home*
*why not share the adventure?*
*Why travel alone?*
*Until then learn:*
*Everything happens when it is meant to happen*
*that is when it is your turn"*

## 80. The Captain

*It is on the darkest night*
*we need the most light*
*to guide us*
*be the Captain inside us...*
*and steer us away*
*before the night leads the soul astray...*

*There are plenty of nights*
*that share no stars or starlight*
*the nights so cold...*
*The soul losing all its wings and the spares too*
*Feeling aged and old and tired...*
*The nights needing light in its hue ...*

*I have been in corners dark...hiding from the darkness of some nights...*
*and then I see a ray...*
*that starts the new day...*
*and I rise again...*
*praying that the day would never come an end...*
*There are nights*
*when I need the most light*

## 81. Songless

How some nights can be?
Both dark and light on my soul and me

I was alone...seeking a warm corner somewhere
and then I heard your heartbeat in my hearts prayer...

How some seasons can be?
Both winter and summer freezing and thawing me

I had a heartful of dreams...and soulful of plans
I've been lost on many a crossroad...but then again I'm just a man
Doing the best I can...
flowing upstream and down
gaining and losing ground at the same time...Bitter sweet wine

How some eyes can be?
Both unkind and ...caring and kind on me...

I have seen the waterfall in your eyes
washing the shadows and shades away
I thought I took the right road so dear life where did I go astray.

You were here and then gone
Now I am songless....I had a song

# 82. Soul to Soul

With my collar turned up...
and my shivering hands deep in my pockets
I was walking ...at a running pace...thru' the park

I crushed a few autumn leaves under my feet...
with no malice or premeditated intentions
trying to escape the fast approaching dark...
Night…
These shortcuts back home are fine in the day
but at night...theses pathways need light...

I wonder if the leaves crushed under my unkind feet
felt fulfilled and complete or wronged and incomplete…

How would they greet the new buds that take their place...?
I have seen year after year
a warm smile on every autumn leaf
and
heard prayers in their tear:
"Bless this day...I may not pass this way
ever again...
Adios Dear Life...Adios Dear friend
I feel fulfilled and complete
Even autumn leaves have heartbeats
Heart to Heart… Soul to Soul
Returning from the parts to the whole"

## 83. Fruit & Seed

*There are no pieces missing...*
*All life is complete indeed...*
*All the answers are contained... in every fruit and seed*

*There are no pieces missing...*
*There are no pieces to throw away...*
*Embrace...with grace and gratitude*
*before the whole jigsaw*
*is boxed away...*
*Dear Life....Embrace every jigsaw...with love and compassion*
*Learn to play...*
*All the jigsaws are complete...*
*"It was I....who missed a heartbeat"*

# 84. Silence is a Language

If I whisper my thoughts...Can you still hear me?
Where are you now?
Are you anywhere near me?

Silence is a language, too...
Ask any yearning eye...lost in the search for something missing...
what is missing?
"All that was...not here
leaving the heart and the soul...fuzzy clear"

Do we need the ears to hear?
How does God listen to all speaking at the same time?
How does he listen to the words and feelings?
Silent unspoken but words said by the heart?

If God listens to one, does he not hear the others?
If he listens to the silence...Who hears the words spoken?
Anyone?... Anywhere?

When I speak in silence to my forefathers...for counsel...
Do they hear?
Do you hear?
Can we hear without the ear?

Can the blind man see the rainbows on the hills?
Can the deaf hear the music of the heart?

How do we attach meaning to what we see and hear?
Dear God...the process is not that clear...
Can you feel what I feel?
What is it that feels our feelings?
How do the feelings grow...or die?
Who changes the canvass in our eyes?

*How we all are connected?*
*Are we connected at all?*
*Or are we just broken bricks and stones in Life's walls?*
*Are all souls truly one day resurrected?*
*How does the soul redeem?*
*How does it dream?*
*What is hope?*
*Explain to me the process...When we lose it and can't cope?*

*How do the hearts that copes...cope?*
*Are they made from a different fibre...thread and rope?*

*Life only gains meaning...when we learn to feel...*
*I was both deaf and blind...*
*Love heals...reveals...seals...*
*Even after a lifetime of draining...*
*there is always more remaining...*

*I know when I whisper my thoughts and prayers...You hear me...*
*What more I can feel...you near me*

## 85. Heart Light

I was out in the rain...raining my pain...
It was taking a long time
I ran out of reasons to stay
and I had lost all my rhymes...

And then in the rain...I felt warm again
I ask how can that be?
Someone somewhere was kind on me...
Someone somewhere...
put some balm in the rain and the air...
I can feel again...
I thought I was beyond repair
But I have healed again...
I have healed again...

I was out in the night...searching for some light...
I searched everywhere…
But the more I searched the more I found
No one really cares...

And then in the night...I saw a candle light
in a doorway no so far
it's taken me half a lifetime
to walk to that doorway from this bar...
Where they serve ale that numbs the scar
and I have healed again
I can feel again
your kind heart and listening ear
has dried away all my tears...

I was out in the day...searching my way
to the door I had long walked past ...
the wrong stays on your mind forever
Oh ...how it lasts and lasts...

I can see the candle light in the night
that is the way I must go
I've taken' my time and fast running out of rhymes
I haven't got much time left to take it slow...
Let me run...And sleep in her sun
and her heart light...tonight

## 86. True

Does anyone seek "something more true"?
"Hands up....
not a soul..."
Dear God the question is:
" These days does anyone seek you?"

Lost ships and sails in the sea...
Somewhere in all the "I's " and " Me's" is me...
searching for me...

These are changing times
these are changing days...
Nothing lasts forever
nothing really stays...
Lost in the daily toil...
in the end...just a mere handful becomes part of life's soil...

No one needs something more true...
Every soul wants something new...
nothing really stays...
in time all perishes away...
Left with empty pages and worn down faces...
We all carry voids and empty spaces...

When was the last you said a prayer...?
Is that your reply:" Who cares?"
These are changing times...
These are changing days...
We are all rushing by
There is no time left to pray...

Let me change the changing times...
This is a new day:
"Dear Life...I am on my knees...Dear God hear me pray"

## 87. When the Night is done

*I have seen you in the sun...*
*I have seen in the starlight...*
*When the night is done*
*I want to sleep in your soul light*

## 88. I Remember

I remember the time
they used to walk together side by side...
Where are those days gone?
Has time and life moved on?

He is almost running...so far apart
what has happened to his heart?
She is struggling to keep pace...
There are questions on her face...
Why?
What have lost from our eyes?
Why do walk so far apart?
What has happened to out hearts?

Should we call it a day?
Or do you want me to stay?
How long can we walk together...apart...this way?
Before the soul questions the heart:
"Tell me the lessons learnt...If we stay?
We have seen better days"

Crossroads are meant to be...When there are changes to our destiny
Breathe deep...Close your eyes...Open your heart to explore
If it is all gone from here...Ask yourself: Gone to which shore?
Sail your soul to that shoreline
and declare: I have come to reclaim what is mine...
Take all my treasures...Take all you need
Take away all the fruit but spare me some seeds
Love is all I need...
If I have truly loved then will always be...with me
I know it never dies...
But some crossroads can mislead the eye
If we have taken the wrong roads somewhere along the way
Let me find where I need to be, today...

Let us walk together again
Side by side
This time around
Let love be our guide

# 89. Sanctus Sanctus

Sanctus…Sanctus
Holy…Holy
Let me say this prayer
and declare to the Universe: "I care…
Blend my heartbeats in to a balm…for those
hearts and souls left in disrepair…
Dear Life…I care…Let me care"

Let me share this plate of food
with deep gratitude
God has been kind on my soul and heart
Left me a generous portion and part…
Let me share it today…
Let me give some away…
Holy…Holy
Sanctus…Sanctus

I am overflowing…
the harvest is rich and growing
I've had more than my share
I have so much spare…
Let me give it away…Let me share today…
Let me share it all today.
Holy…Holy
Sanctus…Sanctus

I don't want my life
to be a gun or a knife…
I just to be
Bandage and balm…and harmony…
I have so much to share
God has been kind…I have so much to spare
Holy…Holy
Sanctus…Sanctus

*All my errors and mistakes*
*were forgiven*
*I've had so many second chances*
*to learn and enrich the way I'm living*
*Let me learn the art...the heart...of sharing and giving*

*Let me sip this glass of wine*
*and remember all that is mine...*
*All the vineyards...and the wine*
*and the sun that shines*
*on all my days...*
*Let me share some away...*
*Let me give some away*
*Holy...Holy*
*Sanctus... Sanctus*

*Let me say this prayer:*
*"Dear Life thank you for your care*
*in all my moments of sadness and disrepair....*
*I can feel again...*
*Let me heal again...*
*All the broken hearts and the lost souls...*
*Let me share some of their tolls...*
*And give love away...Share it all today...Share it all today*
*Holy...Holy*
*Sanctus...Sanctus*

## 90. Add

*Some souls will wing you and make you fly*
*some drain you...badly restrain you and make your spirit die....*
*But you make me fly*
*you bring universe to my eyes.*

*Some hearts will take away all your innocence and make you break*
*some will fill you like a generous waterfall...*
*Fill you with more love than your heart can take...*
*You bring love...You share the ultimate all.*

*Some eyes will drain you....chain you....stain you...restrain you*
*Leaving you...lost in the mind*
*totally blind.*

*Some people only add...sad...*
*And always take away... more than they pay...*
*That's the game they best play*
*best...*
*Leaving your heart and soul in turmoil and unrest...*

*Leaving....sadness... but never a trace of gladness...*

*You are unique...You always...add*
*total joy....pure glad.*
*You make me fly...*
*On the love in your eye*

## 91. I Saw

*It's a beautiful day...*
*Blessed, too...*
*I saw someone special with you...*

*With eyes closed and hands in prayer...*
*I saw you there*
*in the Chapel ...*
*alone*
*on your own...*
*But beware...I also some one else...standing beside you*
*I saw God, there.*
*Listening with his eyes closed and arms around you...all your prayers*

# 92. If

*If you had the chance to live all over again*
*what would you change?*
*Would you take the old jigsaw*
*or would you rearrange?*

*If you were given chance to live your life all over again...*
*What would you do?*
*Would you live the way you lived before...*
*or would you start a new?*

*Next time around...*
*Would you dance differently...?*
*Maybe even try dancing to different music...different sound?*
*Or would you firmly stay on the old familiar ground?*

*Would you take a different road...?*
*A different highway...?*
*Would you try a few new less travelled paths...?*
*A few new byways...?*
*Would you take a different road at the old crossroads...?*
*A different turning...?*
*The last time around did you miss some point?*
*A point of learning...?*

"Dear Life....I have had a beautiful life...
I would not take any different turning ...
the path that I would embrace...
path to higher learning...
I would not change a single thing
I would live just the way I did before...
Dear Life I was blessed
so many kind blessings entered my door...
and embraced me kindly
and sweetly...
I felt blessed...completely...
I pray that I seize life and love
the way I did the life before...
and live and love even more...
and forgive just as easily as I did before...
but the next time even more

I would want everything and everyone
Just like this time around…
Yes…Yes … I confess…
I would plant the same blossoms on my ground"

## 93. Born to Run

I was bred to run...chase the sun...
But look what life has done.
Somehow...I got tied to a plough...

I found love ...
Dear Life I found love...I found home

Then the war...left its scars...
Many died...Many cried...for losses
we all have to carry our crosses.

Soldiers sometimes cry...
when they witness a soldier die...
away from home...on some lonely field
Scars are inflicted and sometimes also revealed...
the salt and balm...
goodwill and harm...
Some soldiers find...
the home they left behind...
And some will never see...their children and family...
I have seen soldiers cry...asking only one question:
"Dear Life...Why? Some wars...leave salt on scars?"

I have found home again...Once again I am
reunited with my long lost friend...
I feel blessed...All my wounds were kindly stitched and dressed...
Back on the fields...I feel re-souled and healed

I found love ...
Dear Life I found love...I found home
The sun is out...Hope it's also there with you....if it isn't
let me know and I shall complain to sunshine

## 94. Shall I Wait

You have left me lonely on a wrong night.
What will you do?
What will you say?
Dear Life I have missed you
I have missed your light...

You missed my call on a wrong day.
What will you do?
What will you say?
Dear Heart If only you knew
How I need you today...

Some mornings are easy...
Some hard to bear...
I wonder if you still care.
Do you still care?

Some nights are wondrous
some just empty space...
I wonder if you still remember my face.
Do you still remember my name?
Do you remember my face?

*You walked away on a wrong road*
*what will you do?*
*What will you say?*
*Dear Life How I wish you turned around*
*and saw me crumble to the ground*
*with a heavy load...*

*Some days are easy to bear*
*some days hard on the soul*
*I been draining...*
*there's less of me remaining...*
*I am all holes...*
*Where is my heart?*
*Where is my soul?*

*What happened and when?*
*What happened to my heart?*
*What happened to my soul?*
*Shall I wait here till you return...the candle still burns?*

## 95. Journey In

I ran to open the door
and sprinted to open the gate...
Hoping ...dearly hoping
that I wasn't late

" Dear Life... I've been waiting...come on in...
If you must journey...journey in to me...beyond the skin...

Stay awhile in the heart...
Flow a little in my eyes
see the universe beyond the skies...
where my soul flies...
Meadows where love grows and never dies...

Come on in...
I've been waiting...
Let the knowing begin...
Know me deeply...Know me completely.

I have seen many travellers
wanting to know no more than the skin...
one in a million souls... who wants to journey in

Let the journey begin
we got time...to make a few more cellars of life's finest wines...

Let me slow it down...
to almost stop...
I am a soul fall
taste me drop by drop...
Dear Life...don't stop...
Come on in...Let the journey begin

Take it slow...as you get to know...me
if you must know me know me deeply...and totally completely

# 96. Ink Drops

What I saw yesterday....left tearfalls in my soul.

Why does it happen what happens sometimes...?
And you try but can't find the words or the reasons
to console the empty in your eyes and heart
And understand what has happened...

When and why does a Mother walk away...?
Does she ever truly turn her back ...
I saw baby duckling suffer a crows attack...
Punctured beyond repair...
God did you see it all...Were you there?
Did you cry any tears...Do you care?

I walked back home with sadness filling all my time and space
I witnessed life show its cold face

I felt numb all day...
kept thinking how the chick passed away...
One moment here...the next moment gone...
The Mother left all alone.

Even today...I can't explain yesterday...
I am still a little fragile when I think...
Can you feel my tears in the ink?
The ink drops are my teardrops

## 97. Move On

*You have left a tear in my eye...*
*How?*
*When?*
*Why?*
*You have left a tear in my eye.*

*You have left my heart wishing...*
*asking...*
*pleading...*
*begging...*
*"Tell me what is missing?"*

*You have left a space in my life...*
*"Caring and kind" is how you describe your knife...*
*You cut away...the empty yesterday*
*and filled it bloom...*
*You have breezed away the gloom...*

*What's missing...is best gone...*
*"Dear Heart ... by the grace of God it's time to move on...Move on*

## 98. Coal in my Soul

I have lost some coal from my soul
I am not sure how.
All I know
I am coal less now...

I have lost some coal from my soul
I am not sure why
All I know
some kind soul is mining in my eye...

There are so many mines...
abundance and rich
there are so many
I can't tell which is which...

There are so many diamonds
in my store.
Some kind heart is leaving more...
why?
"There are mines in your eyes
mines of silver and gold
some new ...some vintage and old
the coal in your soul
Turning to diamonds and more
Overflowing and always adding to the shared shores"

Who are you with a spade in your hand?
"I am making room for the diamonds...
Shovelling the sand..."

There are so many mines in your soul
turned to pure diamonds by your love...what was coal...
You have enriched my soul...

There is no more coal in my soul
Do you know why?
You have turned them all to diamonds in my eye

# 99. Old

I saw her today...
She was clearly...slipping...fading away
shrivelling ...struggling...shivering in her quickly wrapped shawl...
It's amazing how much sand there is in life's wall...
sand that quickly ebbs away...
leaving the bricks to fall away...
from the heart...
how the heart comes apart
as you age and get old...
Dementia can be unkind and cold...

Who is here?
Why is there a glazed eye holding half frozen tear?
How the walls and the castles come apart in the mind...
And a frozen tear...What value does it hold....
From the fragile eye over mined

there's a little black and blue
from her fall
on her own...alone
she called...
No one heard her call...
Every one was away
It's that kind of day...

She lay there...for almost eternity
with one secret fear
Will some one cherish
any of her tears...
or are they...were they...cried in vain?
In the end...What...Who remains?
I see an album of struggle and her sacrifices in her eyes...
But that was in the past...
and the past has no place...in today's skies

I saw her today...
And with a tear in my soul...my heart
almost faded away
Old age ...Dementia...in one purse
I wonder who cares... to reimburse?

# 100. Can J

I look back over all those years
Long ago....He never once complained or shed a silent tear...
Like a soldier duty bound
upright and giving to the last round

Long hours ...long days
seven days...always
at work
to earn
enough to feed the family...and send us to school so we can learn.

"Dad can I have this...Dad can I have that...Dad when will
you buy me this...Dad when...? Dad when...Dad when?"

I never had the sense to see
the man had a rare pedigree...
seven days...sometimes seven nights, too
working...working...as all Dads do...
I should've asked him if he was alright.
Working all those long hours, all those lonely nights...
On his own, So long away from home.

I wish I understood just what he was going thru'
Like all children I never knew
Till one day he collapsed from exhaustion and fell
enough was enough I could tell
and I loudly said
the spirit of this soldier lives on...It is not dead
How can it ever die?
With so many sacrifices in his eyes...
I too am duty bound...
I pray I stay...honourable and a true soldier to the final round...

I wish I understood what my Dad went thru?
But I was only a child...I never knew

"You must learn to forgives the waves
when crossing the sea"...is my Dad once said to me

126

# 101. More

I saw a wave rolling in to the shore...
asking...pleading...
"Is there more....How much more?"

I saw a wave rolling to the shore...
and behind it was another...
followed by a few more
asking....pleading...needing.
"Is there more...I know there's more...
I must touch the countless shores...
and experience the more, more"

I saw a wave rolling back from the shore...
and behind it was another
and a few more
asking...pleading....needing.
"Where is more...Which shore...?
Tell me Dear Sea...I am a new soul...Never been here before...
At least not at your door"

I saw a wave crash back and melt back in to sea
asking...pleading...needing...
"What has happened to me and what I used to be?
Where am I...? Where is me?
I can't see...I am somewhere in the sea...
Which part of the sea is me?
Did I die? Have I died?
When I disappeared somewhere deep inside...the sea...
Which wave is me?
Which wave am I...Dear Life let me know before I die"

I saw a child with tears in his eyes...
asking...pleading...needing
"Are you watching over me from somewhere in the skies?
Have I been raised on lies?
There's a dream in my heart...Bless it with wings...before it wilts and dies"

There are children everywhere
nourished on empty bowls...and a mothers prayer

"Dear Life...Does anyone really care?
Does anyone really share?
Millions of bowls empty...empty as the eyes
when a child dies from hunger...a part of you dies
a part of me dies...
I have walked past many a child...unaware
I didn't see the empty bowl or heard the mothers' prayer...
But later I heard a cry...
when the soul was about to surrender to hunger and die...
I saw a wave come rolling in to the shore...
praying:" let me feel more...
let me see more...let me be more
We all crash back in to the sea...
But before I do...Dear Life...Let me be...more
than I ever been before
and share...
and hear every prayer...
Reach out my hand...to all the waves reaching out to the sand
let me be...the soul you can be proud of, Dear Sea"

## 102. Maybe then

The river changes course and keeps on flowing
But just where or when?
Which meadow it will warm with its cool water
which bank...which bend...which soul...which friend...?
That's the way it goes
that's the way it flows...
Who knows?
When?
It rolls thru' your soul...then, maybe then?

There are hilltops flush with snow
and valleys full of rain...
Some clouds feel they've suffered loses
some clouds feel the gain
that's the way it goes
that's the way it flows...
Who knows?
When?
It rolls thru' your soul...then, maybe then?

Some hilltops are looking empty
as the snow begins to melt
Some hands are best folded
and some played blind to showdown
that's the way some hands are dealt
that's the way it goes
that's the way it flows...
Who knows?
When?
It rolls thru' your soul...then, maybe then?

Some meadows are tended by kind gardeners
some abandoned without care...
Some moments share kind companions
and some left in total disrepair
with not a soul, there
who cares!?

Some hearts do all the forgiving
some never...hardly forgive
some forgive and forget
some carry residue as long as they live...
Some walk with pocketful
some pockets are always empty and in disrepair...
It's these hearts...with pockets empty
who share...I think God lives there...
Some hands are so generous
letting all their diamonds flow with the sand
If I must give my heart and soul away
Dear Life, let me give it to these hands

that's the way it goes
that's the way it flows...
Who knows?
When?
It rolls thru' your soul...then, maybe then
...open your hands....

## 103. Which Road

*Which road?*
*Which way?*
*I am at the crossroads again...so soon...Which way?*
*Turn left ...or right?*
*Go back....or chase the head light?*

*A man can spend all his life... asking question after question at crossroads...*
*But the questions are always the same...*
*Am I a player...Was I ever a player in this game...and what is this game?*
*Invisible crosses on the shoulders...and the soul manoeuvring ball and chain?*

*Let me shed and throw away...*
*All that is excess baggage and just gets in the way...*
*clouding my heart...*
*fogging my eyes...*
*losing truth among excuses and lies....*

*Exactly what are you searching for?*
*"Something truer for sure...*
*Will you be the one...or is this also another wrong door?*

*What lies beyond tonight?*
*What waits beyond today?*
*Are there horizons waiting on me?*
*Or is it best to embrace compromise...and stay?*

*Can you not be truer than the true I know?*
*"Dear Life...What is, is and that's how it sometimes flow*

131

## 104. Threads

*There are four threads in my hand:*
*"Tell me what to do?"*

*"Put them all together*
*and they'll create a different hue*
*And if you hold the threads together*
*they'll add their strength to you…*

*Save all your golden threads*
*don't throw any away...*
*You may need the threads one day, someday….*

*Put all your threads together*
*weave yourself a rope*
*Golden threads*
*of honesty...kindness...love and hope*

*Take the silver thread*
*and wrap it when you tie*
*threads of deep relationships...*
*with someone's eyes*

*Take the golden thread*
*and wrap it around your skin*
*Let the gold unfold*
*the kind soul that soars within*

*Take the weakest thread*
*and weave it in to a rope*
*Hold on Hold On tightly*
*when you feel you're losing both you're grip and hope*

*Take the strongest thread*
*Keep it close as long as you live*
*Let the thread of love*
*also teach you how to forgive*

*All the threads together*
*make a special blend*
*that survives eternity*
*of starts and ends"*

*"Wrap my soul in the threads*
*and my heart in satin sheets*
*Let me feel how it feels*
*to feel wholesome and complete"*

## 105. Attitude of Gratitude

*We spend all our lives...*
*complaining about the clouds that hide the sun...*
*and yet hardly ever thank the blue skies that sometimes sieve thru'*
*to me and you*
*for me and you*

*And so it is with our relationships...*
*We always complain about those who let us down ...*
*or those who turned there back...and walked away...*
*Or those who left us at some forgotten crossroad...*
*And travelled a different road... going home.*

*We hardly ever thank those who stand with us...side by side*
*shoulder to shoulder...*
*back to back...*

*I just want to declare...and shout it out:*
*"Dear Hearts....thank you*
*I owe you a debt of gratitude...*
*You who nourished my soul in love*
*and sweetened my attitude"*

# 106. Equal

I questioned the rainfall this morning:
"Why have you fallen so heavily and for too long?
What if some seedling somewhere isn't strong
Enough to bear
What if they come apart?
And there's no one there ....Who does it turn to for repair?"

"I have fallen only the way I am meant to fall...on all
My purpose is to fall on all...meadows green and deserts dry
There are no callipers in my eye...
Some will embrace my fall
And some hide
The decision is yours
You decide...
I am meant to fall...equally on all"

"Maybe I have judged you unfair...
For that wrong judgement...Let me leave you a prayer
Dear Rainfall when you fall, fall kindly on all"

# 107. I missed the Train today

*Some troubled soul said goodbye*
*to all the illusions and lies*

*I cried*
*when I was told*
*Someone jumped under a train and died.*

*I walked fast to the other station*
*hoping the rain doesn't numb me further...*

*What could be worth more than life?*
*What pots of gold?*
*What ties new or old?*

*What stress or strain?*
*Claimed the remains?*

*Should I cry? I have cried.*

*There should be enough spare hearts and souls*
*to console*
*All the troubled hearts and souls...*
*and embrace them...*
*With kind nursing*
*Count generously what's been taken*
*and be even more kind*
*in reimbursing...*

Let these weary eyes have back
all their dashed hopes and dreams
interwoven with sunshine and moonbeams...
and a stronger rope
interwoven with golden threads of new hope...
and a promise for their eyes
that outlives eternity and never dies...

I wondered whether this person left behind
friends....family...Children....
I wondered whether he realised
how much hope will be taken away today
from their eyes...
I wonder what was on his mind
Was life and love all that unkind?
or does our soul sometimes becomes blind?

I am not sure why I cried but I cried
I don't even know who died...

I cannot hear about souls surrendering...
souls that lose their will and start tendering
souls too weak to put up a fight
I have always believed the soul can conquer
any kind of night...

I think I know why I cried
"There is never a good enough reason to die
so why have you died?"

# 108. Until we fall

Sometimes the lesson is learnt early
some times we don't learn at all
until we fall
until we fall.

Sometimes we seize the moment
sometimes we let it all die
we only notice it
when it all passes by
when it all passes by.

Both life and time are fleeting moments
both have future and past
it is only the now
that doesn't last...
Embrace me kindly
before I, too, fade in to past
now is all we have
Dear Heart make it last...

Sometimes we only dream and wish
sometimes we make it all come true.
Always I wish I knew
how I lost you
how I lost you...
Which dream
Which river and stream
took you away
I wish I can bring back that day
and make it right again
I wish I knew then that it was all to end
Dear Heart...Dear Love...Dear Friend.

Until we fall
we don't realise at all

## 109. Even the Birds

*Even the birds remember the kind faces...and the kind places*
*where they got fed...*
*The kind hands and the generous hearts*
*they stand apart...*

*Even the calm sea...*
*remembered me...*
*the last time I was here...*
*I shared with it a joyful tear...*
*Only a few...add beautiful to Life's hue.*

*The early morning breeze...*
*whistling by...had gratitude in its sighs...*
*the last time I shared my heart and skin...*
*and all the summers of hope within*
*with the shadows on the meadows...*
*the kind shades...*
*where I lay...and stayed...*
*a while...*
*And rising a better man...sharing my smiles.*

*We don't seem to share much...or care much*
*we all simply rush by...*
*Let all our beautiful go unshared...and only when it dies*
*we ask: "Why?"*

## 110. Where does it go?

Lady, won't you tell me
What happens, what really happens
Where does it go?
An easy question
But I still don't know

Lady, won't you tell me
Please tell me, what really happens
When love dies?
Where does it go to, from our eyes?

Won't you tell me?
What happens to the tears?
What happens to the feeling?
When they dry and disappear

How does love, warm and exciting
Sacred and inviting ever start to die?
How does it touch our heart?
How do we say goodbye?
What happens to the feelings?
How do they bring tears to our eyes?

Lady, won't you tell me
What happens, what really happens
How does love die?
Where does it go?
Leaving empty eyes

Oh. It's puzzling me, I need to find out
If love is the reason
How do we live, when we live without?

How does love, warm and exciting
Sacred and inviting ever start to die?
How does it touch our heart?
How do we say goodbye?
What happens to the love?
Where does it go, when it leaves our eyes?

Lady, won't you tell me
What happened, what really happened
When love died?
And moved away from my side?

Lady won't you tell me
Where did it go, did it really die?
Or is it still somewhere, in our weary eyes?

Is love truly eternal?
Or was I told a lie?
Was our love the only love, first to die?

I had it all, I had it all, in the palm of my hands
Yes I had it all; I had it all at my command
Lady won't you tell me...How did it all slip away, like grains of sand

# 111: Half Empty, Half Full

*Why am I always half empty?*
*Why am I never half full?*
*Why am I lying?*
*When I'm not really crying...*
*Who am I fooling, what am I trying to pull.*
*Why can't I be half true?*
*Why am I always half lies?*
*Busy playing games,*
*When I should be ashamed...*
*Best to say nothing and yet I don't even try.*

*Why do I feel distantly closer?*
*Why am I only nearly there?*
*It's all going wrong,*
*My love gets weakly strong.*
*Why am I always in it, only for a share?*
*Why can't I say "I love you"?*
*Why say it "almost nearly ",*
*Like a weathered stone,*
*Used to being left alone,*
*Something's just not right, with my heart clearly.*

CHORUS

*It's time to change and change I will*
*I'm amazed, you love me still.*
*It's time to change and change I will,*
*I'm half empty needing a fill*
*It's time to change my point of view.*
*It's time to change and renew*
*It's time I totally knew.*
*I'm fully in love with you.*

*If I'm half crazy, I must be half sane.*
*Why can't I be always true?*
*Not sure how much remains?*
*Why am I always half lies with you?*
*If I'm half empty, I must be half full,*
*And if I'm half the man I used to be,*
*The better half, remains of me.*
*The other half is ready for the cull...*

CHORUS

*You shared my body, I shared your soul.*
*I dealt in pieces, you dealt in whole.*
*I'm changing for you,*
*And that's the full truth.*

## 112: I can't say no

I better tell you
I've taken, taken all I can
What you put me through
Just wouldn't do, for any other man
So if you want to leave,
Don't threat me, just go
My lips are sealed, I mustn't yield
I can't say no

I got no intentions
To fight the world over you
If you love me, really love me,
There'd be no need to
Your lips are free
To do as they please, stay or go
My lips are sealed, I mustn't yield
I can't say no

Though you're a sure heartache
I just haven't got, what it takes
To let you be, to set you free
And let you go
I'm a jack of losers
And beggars can't be choosers
I can, I can, and I got to say no.

If you go, I wouldn't know
What to live for, and give for, so please
No, I ain't lying
Yes, I've been crying
I'm down on my knees
So if you want to leave
Don't threat me, just go
My lips are sealed
I mustn't yield
I got to say no

## 113: What is "Is" and that's all there "Is"

Some questions have easy answers
Some problems are so easy to solve
Some situations solve themselves
Some you have to resolve
Some happenings can't be explained
No matter how hard you try
You may wonder till the end of time
Some answers always end in why

Well you can think all you like
Some things just happen that way
Things will be what they're meant to be
No matter what you do or say
Some without just reason or rhyme
Some due to the dues to pay
Some happen before their time
And some never see their day

What is, is and that's all there is
Learn to flow
You're holding too tightly
Learn to let go
What is, is and that's all there is
It's the way it's meant to be
Learn to embrace, Grace
Let it be.

Some things, oh when they happen
Seem so out of time and place
But I've learnt in my lifetime
Everything fills only its own space
You can take that for what it is
Or question how that may be
You know you can't change the flow
Each wave has its destiny

## 114: In Lonesome

She says she's free,
For she's thru' with me,
Though she's changed her name,
She'd always remain, Tied to me, In Lonesome.

She says she's free,
To do as she please,
Leaving me broken- hearted
My life has just started, Clearly, In Lonesome.

Funny, I still love her sweetly
But, Honeys got over me completely.

She says she's free,
And she's forgotten me,
Love's gone, I still wait
Knowing the odds, I still anticipate, Dearly, In Lonesome.

I'll always be in debt, how easy we forget.
She says she's free
So, please let things be
Close and move on,
What's over is over and what's gone is gone.

# 115: The Apple Tree

I saw an apple fall free...from the apple tree
Landing on the ground...with not a sound
Quietly laying there...
To see if the ground...or for that matter anyone cared or cares
whispering in a prayer: "Where is the kind hand...
warm balm for the disrepair?"

Sometimes when things fall...no one hears them at all
They just lay there...and no one cares
Sighing...quietly...slowly dying

I saw an apple blossom fall...And I wonder if it fell at all
The kind breeze...kept it in the air...
Long enough to find directions there...
And went on and on...finally falling softly on a kind lawn...
Where a kind heart...picked it up for its fragrance
And held it near her heart...
And felt it never came apart from the apple tree...

"Dear Life you are so kind to me
It is by kind blessing we find love
And by kind blessing we share
It is by kind blessing we find home
And share absolute joy there"
"Dear Life...I have always found love and joy there"

## 116: Its 4am

It's 4 am and the decision is this:
I need to find a way...
I stay awake all night
and sleep all day

I seem to waste my day... So much time has simply slipped away
just what is on your mind?
What is keeping you awake?
"I need to understand the problems
and then correct the mistakes ...
I seem to ignore my mistakes"

"What are these errors you keep referring to?
Some I know and some I wish I knew?
Like most folks...I am trapped between the fire and the frying pan:
What I can't and what I can.
What I should or shouldn't do?
Decisions...Decisions...No wonder I can't sleep
Some problems are shallow...some ocean deep
I need to clear my mind...and un-stress"

"You are clearly over dressed
Take off your jacket...untie the rope
take off the ball and chains ....nearly strangling all your hope
Look up....look up to the sky
That is a must: If you intend to fly
and furthermore...You'll need some wings on your soul for sure
If you got no wings...They can grow just like that
As long as you remember: Everything you need in life is where you're at"

Wishing you all that counts...knowing where it's all at...

# 117: Close to You

Dear Eyes...Rise...and embrace the sunrise
The day is here...
Hold it in your heartbeat...hold it close and near

Dear Eyes...you start my day...
If I don't see you...the day just wastes away
You are my day...

Dear Eyes...you light up the starlight...
and my night...
Dear Eyes you are my light....on a dark velvet night

Dear Eyes...what purpose do I hold
Why was I born...If not to be?
Close to you...
Be close to me…

## 118: When I was young

When I was young...I would jump and catch the moon and a few stars
put them in my pocket
and carry on...
As if Life was still coming...
and nothing was lost or gone...
But these are changing times...
and time has moved on...

When I was young...I felt ageless...timeless...I carried no watch or clock...
I had none in my pocket...or in my buffer stock
I would jump from thought to thought...
believing that I was born forever...
and only the feeble die...
I had that belief in my soul and it reflected that in my eye...
But these are changing times
those days are long gone
and time has moved on...

Now I know even the strong die, too...
something my young heart either never accepted or knew
There is only so much time...
before the vineyard reclaims back it's wine

So while I am still alive....
Let me learn to live and not just survive
Let no one chip away...drain or drip away
my spirit and mind
Let no clinging vine tie me so tightly down
that I drown...
Let me become what I need to become...
Let me complete all the sums...
Let not overload or stress
dismantle and sabotage any of my petals in its press
Let me stay perfectly clear
under any doubt or fear...
Let me soar...and learn more and more...

When I was young I had songs on my tongue
and I sung them all loud
I stood in a crowd and stood out in a crowd
But these are changing times
Now I have become an older wine
Which table, if any, will share when they dine?

Nowadays, I guess I am struggling with the fences and walls...
Have they grown taller...they were never that tall
these are changing times
those days have long gone
and lot of water under the bridge and time has moved on...

But my heart still feels ageless...timeless...no matter what
All else is a passing season...my soul...now that's a matter of fact
Which vineyard am I from?
I feel ageless...timeless as time moves on.

# 119: Cherry Pickings

There are rainbows waiting to be
Cherry picked by you and me
Let us start
With rainbows in our eyes and hope in our heart

Reach out...Reach up
Take a piece of the sky
And rainbow your eye
There are gifts galore...
on every meadow and shore...
Let us start
With kindness in our eyes and abundance in our heart

Reach up...Reach out
Take a piece of the shore
And ocean your door...
Life is just a state of mind...
What you think becomes you
Dear Heart... brush away yesterday and start a new...

There are dreams waiting to be
Cherry picked by you and me
Let us start
With rainbows in our eyes and dreams in our heart

Come sail with me and sail me
Like a kind and gentle breeze guiding me home
And when I cherry pick my rainbows
Let me not be alone...

# 120: Sweet Child of Music

Hey, can't you see, music playing out of me.
Thru' the pours and holes,
Losing my soul,
Let me sing again
As less and less remains... of me ...in the melody

Sweet child of music,
Strum a song into me.
Sweet child of music,
Hum along into me.
Harmonize me,
Lady, make me strong.
Sweet child of music,
Be there to lean on.

CHORUS
Come softly, Come softly,
Come softly, and warm me.
Come gently, Come gently,
Come gently, and calm me.
With love over -flowing
And wild dreams growing.
Child, I can feel it,
Woman, we're getting near it,
Sweet child of music,
Lady, can you hear it.

Sweet child of music,
Lady, Soul in to me.
I can't feel my feelings,
Lady, roll into me
Sweet child of music,
Run into me,
I been living in the shadows,
Child, sun into me

CHORUS
*Come softly, Come softly.*
*Come softly, and play me.*
*Come gently, Come gently,*
*Come gently, and d-jay me.*
*The poetry of my life needs rhyming,*
*It's been clichéd with time, it needs fresh timing.*
*Child, can you feel it,*
*Woman, we're getting near it,*
*Sweet child of music,*
*Lady, can you hear it*

*Sweet child of music, play your songs.*
*I need to hear your music, for mines almost gone.*
*Roll me, rhyme me, re-melody and time me.*
*I'm a soul under strain…as less and less remains…of me*
*And my melody*
*Lady, fill me… before the draining and what's remaining kills me*

## 121: Plans

*Why am I here...?*
*Asking the same question over and over again:*
*"Why ...Dear Heart...Why...Dear Friend"*

*"It's the way it goes...It's the way the river flows...*
*Some things...only heaven knows"*

*Who do I blame...?*
*I don't understand this game:*
*"I wasn't even playing...Why have I lost?"*

*"It's the way it goes...It's the way the river flows...*
*Some things...only heaven knows"*

*How do I tell my heart...?*
*This is not the place or the time to come apart:*
*"Hold on...Hold on Dear Heart"*
*"It's the way it goes...It's the way the river flows...*
*Some things...only heaven knows"*

*The lesson is in the learning...*
*The journey is the prize...*
*Take those lonely teardrops...*
*Left behind for your eyes...*

*Brush away...Wipe your trembling lip and cheek...*
*This is not the place or the time...*
*To expose yourself as fragile or weak...*
*Walk away...and understand...*
*Life runs by its own plans.*

## 122: It is on the Darkest Nights

It is on the darkest of nights
I need the most light
Inside me…to guide me

The night has a way…to lead a soul astray
But today is not that day…

Shine on my soul…
Shine in my eyes…
Be my sun in the sunrise…
I can clearly see…
The night having issues with me …
The light inside me…to guide me

## 123: Hungry Eyes

*My friend saw a child holding an empty plate...*
*standing near her eyes...*

*"Save me ...Save me...*
*It's never too late...*
*there are millions with empty plates"*

*My friend said a prayer...*
*"Dear Life are you there? Be there"*

*My friend...has a kind heart...*
*She always falls apart...*
*Each time she sees a child holding an empty plate*
*near her heart...*

## 124: I'm Still Here

*Tie my heart in prayers*
*let it embrace all my heart beats...*
*I was incomplete*
*Now I feel complete*

*Tie my soul in hymns*
*let it grow strong*
*in assured safety*
*Knowing where it comes from*

*I have travelled a billion miles...*
*I've been around a billion year*
*Reincarnation of soul*
*I've always been here*

*So Dear Life miss me not when I am gone...*
*I am still here...and just moved on*

## 125: Both the Eraser and the Pen

It's amazing how the eye can deceive a man
make all reason and logic leave a man
exactly when he needs them the most
to Solve…Resolve…Define or Dissolve

I saw the rain clouds and could not see
the blue sky anywhere for me…
and I thought that's the way…
the rain clouds can hide any day…away…

and then after the rainfall…
I could not see any rain clouds at all
where did they go?
Are they somewhere behind the sky blue
I wish I knew…?

My eyes see what they see…
but what I see…is that all that's meant to be?
Deception by Perception…
the eye and lens…
acting as both the eraser and the pen

## 126: If I can Offer you

*If I can offer you any learning from my time here...*
*It is: share the smiles and the tears...*
*Don't let any moment emptily pass you by*
*Let all moments...Go thru' your eye...*

*Where is the sense in closing doors...?*
*Let each deep breath...breathe in the whole ocean air...*
*Less is not more only more is more*
*Why waste?*
*Why not taste the ocean from the shore?*

*If there is any learning I can share with you...*
*It is the knowing...the whole purpose of life...is to experience something true*
*Tell me...in all the years that have gone by...*
*From all that has touched you and those who just hastily rushed by...*
*Have you?*

*Do not judge...anything...anyone*
*the weighing scales throw them out...*
*It is the weighing that creates fear and doubt...*
*Just Be....Dear Heart, to just be*
*is the ultimate secret Life has shared with me...*

*So open up...Live and breathe every moment*
*Let it touch your soul and skin...*
*And after...Let it come deep within...*

*Offer Life your deep gratitude...*
*And let that gratitude colour your attitude*

# 127: Come Let us Gather Logs

*Why are you so quiet these days?*
*Which dream has slipped away?*
*I can see the broken threads...*
*tipping the seesaw in your head...*

*Some thoughts can kill a man...*
*some bruise and some still a man...*
*What thoughts are you lost in today?*
*You seem to be slipping away*

*if you must add something to the dying fire...*
*Add only the timber that takes the flames higher...*

*Come let us gather logs...*

*Cut me up and feed*
*all your furnace needs...*
*I am a trunk...branch...a leaf*
*Let me once again make you believe in yourself*
*and take your thoughts away from all else*

*Come let us gather logs...*

## 128: And So, So I Did

It's been coming, pulling near
Coming close and finally it's here
Wanting me, granting me, love

Heaven
Heaven thank the lord
I want to thank you
Heaven
Heaven thank the lord
Oh you know I want to,
Shout
And let this feeling out
As, the fire burnt, I learnt,
My need for you
So, so I did and so, so you did, too

Something warm, yeah something dear
Is what, we got here
The candle's burning and I'm fast learning

All my questions,
Who, Where, When and Why
All the answers are in your eyes
Been searching a lifetime, finally here
Something true, something dear
As I am today, that's how I want to stay.
Changing me, rearranging me
Getting to me
I always knew you already knew me.

*An Afterthought*
*Tomorrow you may say...Where is yesterday?*
*"The day has gone...yesterday has moved on"*

*An Afterthought*
*Dear Life my soul will die...when hope leaves my eye...*
*Let me tie down hope...with all my golden threads and rope...*
*Don't ever let hope die...If it should ever does die, so will I*

# 129: Love into me

Love, sweet love,
Love into me,
Love the way you love
Love the way you're getting to me

And someway
And somehow
And someday
Like right now

Like some good times
Like some reasons and rhymes
Like some sugar and cream
Like some happy dreams

Needing me, truly needing me
And clearly caring
Get to know me deeply
So both my heart and soul shakes
With you getting to know me
Getting to know me completely

Love, sweet love
Love into me
Love the way you love
Love the way you love into me

*And sad days*
*Seen me plenty*
*Not today*
*Love wants me*

*Like some barefoot walks*
*Like some contented talks*
*Like some warm easy smiles*
*Like you honey child*

*Ah run into me*
*Take the shadows*
*And sun into me*

*Take your time and explore*
*There is so much more*
*Love into me*
*Stay, don't quickly journey thru' me*

# 130: Canto Libri

I saw a butterfly in the distance
quietly kissing all the flowers
afraid the day maybe over soon
so it stayed a few more hours...

"Winter can be too long
and the summer too brief
I have spent many seasons
on fallen crumbling leaf...
Some hearts wait forever never sure
what they're waiting on has maybe already left and gone
After knocking on their door...
Slow down dear heart...it is time to see
the detail left by time in hazy me"

I saw a robin sitting on a lilac tree
asking only one question:
"Are all these blossoms just for me?"
Some blossoms are meant to wither
Unnoticed and untouched
And some are meant to be
Dear Life which blossoms were sent for me?
And meant for me?

I have seen many blossoms before
but none fell near my door...
Slow down dear heart it is time to see
if any season has left their blossoms in me?
Some blossoms fall near and get blown away
Dear Heart it is love that makes them stay"

*Collection of quiet thoughts, smiles and teardrops, seasons and reasons...*
*Collection of heart beats and their sighs left by*
*changing times and life's blessings...*
*Collection of moments, fragments assembled in to a rosary*
*of stones and diamonds, pebbles and pearls...*

*My songbook, my heartbeats, my prayers, my moments of glory and*
*tears, my moments of being together and alone, lonely and loved,*
*cherished and ignored, fragmented and put together again, broken and*
*assembled perfectly, embraced and pushed away, winter and summer,*
*autumn and springtime....my moments of deserts and meadows*
*green...my time with you and time away from you, my moments*
*of clarity and perfect understanding and unsure crossroads,*
*my songbook, my soul exposed, my searching days, my found days.*

*"The morning rain has been quietly falling*
*on my sun-burnt ageing skin*
*Some raindrops are seeping in*
*Thru' skin fragile and thin.*

*Some raindrops were kind and warm*
*And some unfairly, fairly unkind*
*Some fell quietly on my skin*
*And some went straight for the mind.*

*Some fell quietly*
*combing my too often spring breeze-kissed hair*
*falling in time and harmony*
*with the bible in my heart and the soul in my prayer...*
*Dear Life...can you feel all of me there"*

# Epilogue

All story books have an ending, the ending
comes with a finding…Absolute joy.

I hope these pages were kind on my thoughts and that
you shared the thoughts and journey standing with me
in the centre of my life and not just the edge.

I too have shared in others journeys and felt the intensity of
their needs and so dedicate the thoughts within this book to the
children who receive kind treatment at the Great Ormond Street
Hospital Charity (London, UK) with love I pledge to donate
half of the income proceeds of this book to their noble cause.

The Great Ormond Street Hospital Charity deals with
192,000 patient visits every year and they are extraordinary
in the way they "put the child first always".

I feel blessed that I can do this and I feel even more blessed knowing
that you have been kind companions on that journey with me.

# About the Author

**Birri Sangha** captures human emotions with warmth, understanding and sensitivity. His main passion is to understand the meaning of life through the arts, rich literature, philosophy, music and life sciences. A prolific writer, who attempts to capture life's moments in words of warmth, compassion and empathy.

His other work published and due in publication include:

Shishya
Stillpoint
PS I Love You
Errors of Salience
Warm Skin of Now
Shadows on the Meadows
Heartbeats in the Eye
Soul at a Soul Crossing
Canto Libri

Lightning Source UK Ltd.
Milton Keynes UK
UKOW051948250712

196567UK00002B/3/P

9 781477 214671